UPANISHADS
Made Easy to Understand

With illustrations, abstract, explanatory rendering (**without Sanskrit verses**) of all verses in simple, modern English; copious notes and gloss on difficult verses and words; simpler, important verses are printed in **Highlighted-bold** for the first time readers; 83 quotations from the Bhagavad-Gita; Chapter&Section headings, Glossary of Sanskrit words used, Cross Reference, A meditation technique.

Ramananda Prasad, Ph.D.

Our Publications List: www.gita-society.com/books.html
Buy this book from: www.amazon.com/dp/1497300142
Buy Chhandogya& Brihadaranyak Upanishads from:
www.amazon.com/dp/1530172195
Buy this book in Hindi: www.amazon.com/dp/1515273326

INTERNATIONAL GITA SOCIETY

A Preview

"… Dr. Prasad's deft rendering of the nine principal Upanishads with subsidiary supports **makes an in-road and gives access to the magnificent conclusions left by the ancient sages of India.** This book gives us a summary view of the information which was divulged by those teachers. It's easy to read and understand and will encourage you to delve deeper into the subject matter."

— Michael Beloved, New York

LIST OF ABBREVIATIONS USED

01. IsU   Ishāvāshya Upanishad
02. KeU   Kena Upanishad
03. KaU   Kaṭha Upanishad
04. PrU   Prashna Upanishad
05. MuU   Mundaka Upanishad
06. MaU   Māndukya Upanishad
07. TaU   Taittiriya Upanishad
08. AiU   Aitareya Upanishad
09. ShU   Shvetāshvatara Upanishad

10. ChU   Chāndogya Upanishad
11. BrU   Brihadāranyaka Upanishad
12. RV   Rigveda
13. YV   Yajurveda
14. SV   Sāmaveda
15. AV   Atharvaveda
16. BG   Bhagavad-Gita, 83 Quotes
17. MB   Mahābhārata
18. BP   Bhāgavata Purāna

Read all references to Gita verses in this book in:

www.gita-society.com/explanationRead.html

For a **Glossary** of Sanskrit words used:

www.gita-society.com/glossary-up.doc

Contents

Customer Reviews on amazon.com:

www.gita-society.com/books.html
Showing 1-4 of 4 reviews(5 star).
To buy this book:-- www.amazon.com/dp/1494922398

Ana Santos
5.0 out of 5 stars Understand what you're reading
Reviewed in the United States on April 11, 2019
Format: Paperback Verified Purchase
Been learning about upanishads on YouTube. Then after reading this book I
know what I was reading.
I can't tell you if some kind of spiritual affect was happening. But I can tell you
that that just knowing about
 it made me happy.
4 people found this helpful

> Mark this review as helpful BUTTON

LP
5.0 out of 5 stars like the Bhagavad Gita
Reviewed in the United States on January 19, 2018
Format: Paperback Verified Purchase
Ah, the essence of Sanatam Dharma, aka Hinduism. The foundational
understanding of reality, self and God.
The Upanishads, like the Bhagavad Gita, are the essence of Veda and all
religions, in my opinion.
A must have for all human beings!
4 people found this helpful

> Mark this review as helpful BUTTON

5.0 out of 5 stars nice book to have
Reviewed in the United States on April 16, 2015
Format: Paperback Verified Purchase
i bought this book because i enjoying reading the upanishads. this book adds to
my collection and more detailed description. nice book to have. highly
recommend this book.
4 people found this helpful

Mark this review as helpful BUTTON

2 people found this helpful
Robin
5.0 out of 5 stars as advertised
Reviewed in the United States on November 3, 2015
Format: Paperback Verified Purchase
good for beginners interested in Hinduism

i bought this book because i enjoying reading the upanishads. this book adds to my collection and more detailed description. nice book to have. highly recommend this book.
4 people found this helpful

Mark this review as helpful BUTTON

2 people found this helpful

Robin
5.0 out of 5 stars as advertised
Reviewed in the United States on November 3, 2015
Format: Paperback Verified Purchase
good for beginners interested in Hinduism
         ****

This book is meant for the first time readers who have studied Gita and have some familiarity with Vedic culture, religion and Sanskrit words. Advanced study of the Upanishads should be pursued by "sitting down near a qualified spiritual master.

ISBN13: 978 149 730 0149
ISBN10: 149 730 0142

CONTENTS

Contents

Contents

INTRODUCTION

The philosophical portion of the Vedas is called the Upanishads. The Upanishads are found mostly in the concluding part of the Vedas and are also called Vedānta (added at the end of the Vedas). They are found appended to all the four Vedas, and thus we have Upanishads belonging to all four Vedas: Rig, Yajur, Sāma and Atharva. Each Vedas reveals its contents under four sections: **(1)** The **Samhitās**, containing beautiful lyrical poems or **mantras** describing and adoring the beauty of nature and the power of the extraordinary forces. **(2)** The **Brahmanas** section containing the **ritualistic injunctions** and prescriptions for various ceremonies. **(3)** The Aranyakas, containing various methods of worship **or Upāsanās** and (4) The **Upanishads**, containing the philosophical discussions and sermons that had taken place at various periods of time between different teachers (Rishis) and their students, regarding Brahman, Eternal Purpose of creation and the goal of human life. While the hymns of the Vedas emphasize rituals and the Brahmanas serve as a manual for those Vedic rituals. The Upanishads are inherently opposed to rituals.

The name 'Upanishad' has a very purposeful meaning and deep significance. The Sanskrit word Upanishad translates to: "Upa (near) ni (down) shad (sit), sitting down near a teacher". The term 'Upanishad' literally means sitting near the enlightened Master and listening closely to the mystic doctrines of the spiritual teacher, who has grasped the fundamental truths of the universe. To Indian scholars 'Upanishad' also means a literature that destroys our present ignorance of Reality and helps the student to attain the Supreme Knowledge. There are more than 200 known Upanishads, one of which, Muktikā Upanishad, predates 1656 and contains a list of 108 authorized Upanishads, including itself as the last. The first dozen out of 108 Upanishads are the oldest and most important known as the principal Upanishads. They all predate 6th century BCE. The top **Nine Principal Upanishads** are introduced in this book in simple, easy to understand modern English.

1. ISHĀVĀSHYA UPANISHAD

ॐ पूर्णमदः पूर्णमिदं, पूर्णात् पूर्णमुदच्यते
पूर्णस्य पूर्णमादाय, पूर्णमेवावशिष्यते
ॐ शान्तिः शान्तिः शान्तिः

Om! purnamadah purnamidam,
purnāt purnam-udacyate.
purnasya purnamādāya,
purnam-eva-avashishyate.

Om! Shantih! Shantih! Shantih!

Om! The invisible Brahman is infinite; the visible Universe is also infinite. From infinite Brahman, infinite universes come out and dissolve in. The infinite Brahman still remains infinite, even though infinite universes come out and go in it.

Read an explanation of this very important verse:

www.gita-society.com/purna-madah.html

The **Ishāvāshya Upanishad** is one of the shortest of the Upanishads. It is more like a short poem than a philosophical treatise, consisting of only **18 verses in poetry.** This Upanishad constitutes the final chapter of the Shukla Yajurveda. The study of Upanishads traditionally starts with this Upanishad and should go on in the sequence given in this book.

All is Brahman

ॐ ईशा वास्यमिदं सर्वं, यत्किञ्च जगत्यां जगत् ।
तेन त्यक्तेन भुञ्जीथा, मा गृधः कस्यविद् धनम् ॥

Om! Ishāvāsyam idam sarvam, yatkincha jagatyām jagat.
Tena tyaktena bhunjithā, mā gridhah kasyavid dhanam.

01. Whatever exists in this transient world is an abode (वास) of Lord of the universe (Isha, God). Enjoy what is given to you by the Lord—with a spirit of renunciation (Samnyāsa) that nothing belongs to you, but to God. Do not crave for material possessions. (Also see BG 7.19)

After many births, the enlightened one surrenders to My Will by realizing that everything is, indeed, My manifestation. Such a great soul is very rare. **(BG** 7.19) (Also see **BG** 7.07, **18.**66)

The other seven Sanskrit verses of the Vedas, called great sayings (महावाक्य) are: **(1)** All this is, of course, the Spirit because everything is born from, rests in, and merges into the Spirit (सर्वं खल्व् इदं ब्रह्म in ChU 3.14.01 of Sāmaveda). **(2)** All this is Spirit. The Spirit is everywhere. All this universe is, indeed, Supreme Brahman (ब्रह्मैवेदं विश्वमिदं वरिष्ठम्) in MuU 2.02.11 of Atharvaveda. The Bible also says: You are gods (John **10.**34). The Vedas and Upanishads declare: **(3)** Consciousness is Brahman (प्रज्ञानं ब्रह्म in AiU 3.03 of Rigveda). **(4)** I am the Spirit (अहम् ब्रह्मास्मि in BrU 1.04.10 of Yajurveda). **(5)** You are the Spirit (तत् त्वम् असि in ChU 6.**08.**07 of Sāmaveda). **(6)** The individual Self (Jivātmā, Jiva) is one and the same as the Absolute (Brahman, Brahma) (अयम् आत्मा ब्रह्म in MaU 02 of Atharvaveda) and **(7)** That which is One has become all these (इदं विबभूव सर्वम् in Rigveda 8.58.02).

Because of being beginningless and unaffectable by the three modes of material Nature, the eternal Supersoul—even though dwelling in the body as a living entity—neither does anything nor becomes tainted by Karma, O Arjuna. **(BG 13.**31)

The universe is made up of the Lord (सीयाराम मय). He is the creator, operator and destroyer. The universe is made up of God, made by God, and made for God to reside, play and enjoy His own creation by becoming jivātmā.

Live Like a Lotus Leaf

02. People should wish to live full life span (of 100 years) **by doing their prescribed duty (without ego and attachment to results). There is no other way to avoid the bondage of karma.**
The Bhagavad-Gita also says:

One who does all work as an offering to God—abandoning attachment to results—remains untouched by karmic reaction or sin, just as a lotus leaf never gets wet by water. **(BG** 5.10)

Destiny of the Ignorant

03. Those devoid of Self-knowledge, also called the slayers of Ātmā (आत्महन्ता), are verily born in the wombs of evil beings, lacking Self-knowledge, after death.

I hurl these cruel, sinful, and mean people, into the cycles of death and birth in the womb of demons (or degraded parents) again and again, according to their karma. **(BG 16.**19)

Description of the Un-Describable Ātmā

04. Ātmā appears Immovable (अचल), yet it remains in constant motion (अत्, चल)**. It is swifter than mind and beyond the reach of intellect, always remaining ahead of mind and senses (*because it carries mind and senses with it*). Thus, Ātmā out runs all those who run. The cosmic energy of Ātman, the Prāna, sustains activities of living beings; Ātman really does no action.

**The electrons and protons are in constant motion. This motion is what we call 'RāsaLilā' of Krishna, the never ending dance of Prakriti and Purusha.

05. Ātmā moves and also does not move; it is very far as well as very near. It is both inside and outside all beings. (Also see **BG 13.**15)

The Beauty of Advaita Philosophy

06. The wise one perceives one's own higher Self in all, and all in one's own higher Self. Therefore, he does not hate or injure anyone. Such a person loves everybody as one loves God.

07. The wise one who has realized that his own higher Self has become all, and sees the oneness of entire existence (अद्वैत, non-dual), what sorrow and what delusion can overwhelm him?

One, who sees One in all and all in One, sees the One everywhere and in everything. To fully understand this and to experience the oneness of individual soul and the Supersoul, is the highest achievement and the only goal of human birth.

How to Work and Worship

08. He (the Self) is all-pervading, radiant, bodiless, spotless, all-powerful, pure, untouched by sin and all-seeing, all-knowing, transcendent, and self-existent. He assigns duty and properly gives the fruits of one's karma.

Reconciliation of Contradictions

09. Into the blinding darkness enter those who practice Avidyā (rituals, fruitive actions, कर्मकाण्ड) only; and into greater darkness those who practice Vidyā (or seek theoretical Knowledge, ज्ञानकाण्ड) only.

He who worships deities (many gods) to fulfill material desires is in the mode of passion (Rajas). Such a person is ignorant like a child, because he thinks: I am different from God (द्वैतभाव). Pursuit of only theoretical Vedic knowledge without any action is useless and is in the mode of greater ignorance (Tamas). There is no doubt that twelve years of Vedic study had left Shvetaketu both ignorant, proud and arrogant (ChU 6.1.03).

10. One thing, they say, is obtained from Vidyā (Jnāna or Gnāna) and another thing from Avidyā (karma). Thus we have heard from the wise who have taught us this.

11. One who pursues both Avidyā and Vidyā together, attains relative immortality—by going to heaven where there is no fear of death—by Avidyā or good karma, and obtains immortality by Vidyā, the Self-knowledge.

The idea behind verses 9, 10 and 11 is that one must not neglect either karma or Jnāna. The fruit of Gnāna can only come out from the soil of karma, therefore, karma is better than mere book knowledge. **(BG** 5.02). But, both are complementary and not exclusive or contradictory as some may believe. (Also see **BG 18.**78)

12. Into a blind darkness enter they who worship manifest god or a deity (असंभूति, साकार ब्रह्म, क्षर पुरुष, द्वैत, अविद्या) only (just to fulfill desires, without knowing that deities are not God). But into a greater darkness enter they who worship formless, Brahman (संभूति, निराकार ब्रह्म, अक्षर ब्रह्म, अद्वैत, विद्या) only. (Also see KeU 1.05)

The Bhagavad-Gita says: Self-realization is more difficult for those who fix their mind on the impersonal and formless Absolute, because worship of the impersonal is difficult for ordinary human beings and the beginners. **(BG** 12.05). Shri Ramakrishna said: "Image worship is necessary in the beginning, but not afterwards, just as scaffolding is necessary during the construction of a building."

13. One thing, they say, is obtained from knowledge of the manifest Brahman; another, they say, from Knowledge of the unmanifest Brahman. Thus we have heard from the wise who taught us this.

14. He who worships (realizes or fully understands) both the un-manifest and the manifest Brahman, overcomes fear of death in the heaven by the worship of deities (manifest, साकार, असंभूति) and obtains immortality by true Knowledge of the Absolute, formless, non-dual, Brahman (un-manifest, निराकार, संभूति).

To those who worship Me meditating on My personal form with unswerving devotion, setting Me as their supreme goal, offering all actions to Me—I swiftly become their savior from the world that is the ocean of death and transmigration. (Also see KaU 6.13, BG 12.06-07)

The ideas behind verses 12, 13 and 14 are that one must very well worship or understand both sides (or aspects)—the personal and the impersonal—of the coin of Reality. The Absolute Being is beyond the human conception of form and formless. It has a transcendental form beyond human conception of form and formless. **(BG** 7.24).

Nirvāna by Giving Up the Ego

15. The face of Truth is covered with a golden curtain of ego (maya, ignorance). Uncover it, O (Sun) God, so that I, who am devoted to the Truth, may behold it!

16. O Pushan, the nourishing God in the form of Sun, O controller and supporter of all, withdraw your blinding radiance of ignorance; and focus your soothing rays of Gnāna on me, so that I may be able to comprehend Your transcendental form. And realize that whosoever person is up there, that also I am (सोऽहम्).

Always Remember God

17. Now, let my breath be merged in all-pervading immortal Prāna, and the body be reduced to ashes. O mind! remember Om!, remember past deeds. The mind remembers all that I have done. (Also see BG 8.06–07)

During the last moment of our life, the mind automatically remembers what we have done during the entire life, as mentioned in **BG** 8.06.

Rishi Ghora Āngirasa, communicated the following teaching to his student, Krishna, the son of Devaki—and it quenched Krishna's thirst for any other knowledge. Rishi said: "When a man approaches death he should take refuge in these three last thoughts: "Om! Thou art indestructible," "Thou art unchanging," and "Thou art the subtle essence of Prāna." (ॐ त्वं अक्षितं असि, त्वं अच्युतं असि, त्वं प्राणसंशितमसि) (ChU 3.17.06)

18. O Agni (the Bright Being)! Lead us to blessedness by the noble path—the **Northern path** of gods. O Lord! You know all our deeds, remove all evil and delusion from us. To Thee we offer our prostrations and prayers again and again.

Note 1: The Northern path—the path of no return—has been also mentioned in the Upanishads (**ChU** 4.15.05, **BrU** 6.2.15, **BG** 8.24-26)

OM TAT SAT

2. KENA UPANISHAD

ॐ सह नाववतु ।

सह नौ भुनक्तु ।

सह वीर्यं करवावहै ।

तेजस्वि नावधीतम् अस्तु ।

मा विद्विषावहै ॥

ॐ शान्तिः शान्तिः शान्तिः

Oṁ saha nāvavatu

Saha nau bhunaktu

Saha vīryaṁ karvāvahai

Tejasvi nāvadhītam astu

Mā vidviṣāvahai

May He protect us both (the teacher
and the pupil). May He nourish us both.
May we work together with great vigor.
May our study be thorough and fruitful.
May we never misunderstand each other.

Om! Shantih! Shantih! Shantih!

The Kenopanishad is one of the earlier primary Upanishads. It is associated with the Sāmaveda where it is found inserted into the last section of the Jaiminiya Upanishad Brahmana. It discusses how our senses get their power from Brahman. Brahman is the unknown and unknowable. Everything runs by the power of God, Devas (gods) also get their power from Brahman. The Sanskrit word 'Kena' means by whom. It has **35 verses written in prose.**

CHAPTER 1. KNOWLEDGE OF BRAHMAN

1.01. The disciple asked: Om! By whose will does the mind proceed to its objects? At whose command does the Prāna do its duty? At whose will do men utter speech? Who directs the eyes and ears to function?

Brahman Powers Our Senses

1.02. The teacher replied: it is the spirit (Ātmā) by whose power the ear hears, the eyes see, the tongue speaks, the

mind understands and Prāna function. **Having distinguished the Self from the non-Self (body, mind, sense-organs), the wise attains immortality.**

1.03-04. The eye does not go there, nor speech, nor the mind. We do not know it, nor do we know any method of instructing about it. It is different from everything known; it is unknowable. Thus we have heard from the teachers who taught it to us.

1.05. That which cannot be expressed by speech, but by which speech is expressed, know that alone as Brahman, and not what people here worship.

Note 2: People worship deities or some extra-cosmic Being to fulfill desires. These deities are not Brahman. Lord Krishna said: O Arjuna, even those devotees who worship the deities with faith, they also worship Me, but without proper understanding (9.23).

1.06. That which cannot be comprehended by the mind, but by which the mind comprehends, know that alone as Brahman, and not what people here worship.

1.07. That which cannot be seen by the eye, but by which the eye sees, know that alone as Brahman, and not what people here worship.

1.08. That which cannot he heard by the ear, but by which the ear hears, know that alone as Brahman, and not what people here worship.

1.09. That which cannot be smelt by the breath, but by which the breath smells, know that alone as Brahman, and not what people here worship.

CHAPTER 2. BRAHMAN IS UNKNOWABLE

2.01. The teacher said: If you think: "I know Brahman well," then surely you know very little about it. You only know it as perceived by human mind. Therefore you should enquire further about Brahman.

2.02. The disciple said: I think I know Brahman, but very little. I do not think I know it well, nor do I think I do not know it. He among us who knows the meaning of "Neither do I not know, nor do I know"—knows Brahman. (Jivātmā does has very limited Knowledge of Brahman.)

Brahman is Unknown to the Wise

2.03. The teacher said: He by whom Brahman is not known, knows it; he by whom it is known, does not know it. It is unknown by those who know it; it is known only by those who do not know it.

(Brahman is unknown to the wise and known only to the ignorant, अविज्ञातं विजानतां, विज्ञातम् अविजानताम्)

2.04. Brahman is known when it is realized as a witness in all the three (waking, dream and deep sleep) states of consciousness (see MaU 01-06); by such Knowledge one attains immortality and strength to face all difficulties and fear of death.

2.05. If a man knows Ātmā in this life, he then attains the true goal of human birth. If he does not know it in this life, a great calamity awaits him. **Having realized the Self in every being, the wise renounce the illusory world and become immortal.**

CHAPTER 3. BRAHMAN RUNS THE UNIVERSE

Everything Runs by The Power of God

3.01. Brahman, according to the story, got a victory for Devas over Asuras (demons); and by that victory (of Brahman) the gods became elated. They said to themselves: "Verily, this victory is ours; verily, this glory is ours only."

All actions are actually performed by various forces (or Gunas) of Nature, but due to delusion of ego or ignorance, people assume themselves to be the sole doer and get bound by karma. (BG 3.27)

3.02. Brahman, knowing their pride born out of ego (The ego is a notion that oneself, instead of God, does all works!), appeared before them as a male spirit (Yaksha). But gods did not know who that adorable Spirit was.

3.03-06. They said to Agni (Fire god): "O Agni! Find out who this great Spirit is. "Yes," he said, and hastened to it. Brahman asked him: "Who are you?" He replied: "I am known as Agni." Brahman said: "What power is in you?" Fire replied: "I can burn all—whatever there is on earth." Brahman put a dry straw before him and said: "Burn this." He rushed toward it with full force but could not burn it. When he returned from the visit with this Spirit and said to the other gods: "I could not find out who this Spirit is."

3.07-10. Then they said to Vāyu (Air god): "O Vāyu! Find out who this great Spirit is. "Yes Sir," he said and hastened to it. Brahman asked him: "Who are you?" He replied: "I am known as Vāyu." Brahman said: "What power is in you that make you great?" Vāyu replied: "I can carry off all—whatever there is on earth." Brahman put a dry straw before him and said: "Carry this." He rushed toward it with full force but could not move it. Then he returned from the Spirit and said to the gods: "I could not find out who this Spirit is."

3.11-12. Then the gods said to Indra: "Indra Bhagavān! Find out who this great Spirit is. "Yes," he said and hastened to it. But the Spirit disappeared from him. Then Indra saw in that very region of the sky a Woman highly adorned. She was Umā Devi, the daughter of the King of Himalayas. He approached Her and said: "Mother! who that great Spirit could be?"

CHAPTER 4. THE GLORY OF BRAHMAN

Devas Get Power from Brahman

Devi instructs Indra about Brahman

4.01. Mother replied in great detail: "It was, indeed, Brahman. Through the victory of Brahman alone you have attained glory." After that Indra understood that it was Brahman and realized his mistake and learned a lesson.

4.02. Since these Devas came very near Brahman and were the first to know Brahman. These three Devas, namely: Indra, Agni, and Vāyu excelled the other gods.

4.03. Since Indra approached Brahman and he was the first to know Brahman, Indra excels the other gods and is considered the King of gods.

4.04. This is the description of Brahman with regard to the gods: Devas get power from Brahman. Brahman is behind every form of power, movement and life (Prāna) in the universe.

4.05. Now the description of Brahman with regard to the individual self: **Because of the powers of Brahman, the mind knows the external world, remembers, creates and imagines things.**

4.06. That Brahman is called the adorable of all; it should be worshipped by all. **All creatures love him who worships (or realizes) Brahman.**

The Teachings of Upanishad Lead to Liberation

4.07. The disciple said; "Teach me, sir, the Upanishad." The teacher replied: "I just now told you the Upanishad about Brahman." But I will repeat again:

4.08. Austerities, self-restraint, and sacrificial works are its feet, and the Vedas are all its limbs. Knowledge is its abode.

4.09. He who thus knows this Upanishad shakes off all sins and becomes firmly established in the Infinite. He reaches the main goal of human birth.

OM TAT SAT

3. KAṬHA UPANISHAD

ॐ असतो मा सद्गमय
तमसो मा ज्योतिर्गमय
मृत्योर्मा अमृतं गमय
ॐ शान्तिः शान्तिः शान्तिः

Oṁ asato mā sad gamaya
Tamaso mā jyotirgamaya
Mṛtyormā amṛtaṁ gamaya
Oṁ śāntiḥ śāntiḥ śāntiḥ

Om! Lead me from unreal to real,
lead me from darkness to light.
lead me from death to immortality,
Om! Shantih! Shantih! Shantih! **(BrU 1.3.28)**

The Katha Upanishad is also titled "Death as a Teacher". It is one of the primary Upanishads and is associated with the Krishna Yajurveda. It has **119 verses in poetry.**

THE STORY OF NACHIKETĀ

SECTION 1. NACHIKETĀ IS NOT AFRAID OF DEATH

1.01. Rishi Uddālaka, the son of maharishi Aruna, desiring heaven, performed the Vishvajit sacrifice, in which he gave away all his property. He had a son named Nachiketā.

1.02–03. When the gifts were being distributed, faith entered into the mind of Nachiketā, who was still a boy. He said to himself: Joyless are the worlds to which he goes who gives away cows that no longer are able to drink, to eat, to give milk, or to give a calf.

Nachiketā's felt very compassionate for his father. Thus to save his father from the sin of giving such a fake donation, he presented himself as a real object of donation and said to his father:

1.04. Father! To whom will you give me? He repeated this a second and a third time. Then his father angrily replied: To death I will give you.

1.05. Nachiketā thought: Among some of the followers of my father, I am the first; or among many I am the middlemost. But certainly I am never the last. What work of Yama, the King of Death, will be accomplished by my father giving me away to Yama?

1.06. Look back and see how the ancients honored their promise at any cost. Like corn, the mortals ripen and fall and are born again. Thinking like this, Nachiketā decided to go to Yama.

Nachiketā's father really did not want him to die, but to make the words of his father true, Nachiketā convinced his father to allow him to go to Yama.

Nachiketā in the House of Death

The first test of Nachiketā

Yama was not at home when Nachiketā arrived. He waited for three days without any food or water. Upon Yama's return, Yama said thus:

1.07. Like fire, when a Brāhmana guest enters a house; the householder pacifies him by giving him water and a seat.

1.08. The Brāhmana, who stays in a house without a meal, destroys that foolish householder's hopes and expectations, the reward of his good associations, the merit of his beneficial speech, the good results of his sacrifices and beneficial deeds and all his cattle and children as well.

Three Wishes Offered to Nachiketā

1.09. Yama was very pleased with Nachiketā's firm determination and said: O Brāhmana, salutations to you! You are a venerable guest and have dwelt in my house three nights without a meal; therefore now choose your three wishes, one for each night, O Brāhmana

Nachiketā's First Wish
Return to an Appeased Father on Earth

1.10. Nachiketā said: O Death, may my father, be calm, cheerful and free from anger toward me! May he recognize me (not as ghost!) and welcome me when I shall be sent home by you! This I choose as the first of the three wishes.

1.11. Yama said: Through my favor, your father will recognize you and be again toward you as he was before. After having seen you freed from the jaws of death, he will sleep peacefully at night and bear no fear against you.

Nachiketā's Second Wish
Understanding of the Sacrificial Fire

1.12. Nachiketā said: In the Heavenly World there is **no fear of death** and no one is afraid of **old age**. There one rejoices leaving behind both **hunger and thirst** and is out of the reach of **sorrow**.

1.13. You know, O Death, the fire-sacrifice, which leads to Heaven. Explain it to me. The inhabitants of heaven attain immortality. This I ask as my second wish.

1.14. Yama said: I know the fire-sacrifice well, which leads to Heaven and I will explain it to you. Listen to me. Know this to be the means of attaining Heaven. It supports the universe; it dwells in the causal hearts of the wise who know it.

1.15. Yama then told him about the fire, which is the source of the worlds and what kind of bricks and how many were to be gathered for the altar and how many and how the sacrificial fire was to be lighted. Nachiketā memorized all that was told to him. Then Yama, being pleased with him, spoke again.

1.16. Death, being well pleased, said to Nachiketā: I will now give you another wish: This fire-sacrifice shall be named after you. Take also from me this beautiful chain.

1.17. He who has performed this Nachiketā fire sacrifice three times, has read the three Vedas and also has performed his three duties (Dharma, Artha and Kāma), overcomes birth and death. Having known this fire-sacrifice disclosed to me by the omniscient, luminous and adorable Brahman, one attains supreme peace.

1.18. He who has performed the Nachiketā sacrifice three times; becomes free from fear of death in this life, overcomes grief and rejoices in Heaven.

1.19. This, O Nachiketā, is your fire-sacrifice, which leads to Heaven and which you have chosen as your second wish. People will call this Fire by your name. Now, O Nachiketā, choose the third wish.

Nachiketā's Third Wish
Knowledge of life after death

1.20. Nachiketā said: There is this doubt about a man when he is dead: Some say that he exists; others say he does not exist. This I would like to know from you. This is the third of my wishes.

Yama tests Nachiketā again

1.21. Yama said: On this subject even the gods formerly had their doubts. It is not easy to understand. The nature of Ātmā is very subtle. Therefore, choose another wish, O Nachiketā! Do not press me. Release me from this favor.

1.22. Nachiketā said: O Death, even the gods have their doubts about this subject; and you have also declared it to be not easy to understand. But another teacher like you cannot be found and surely no other wish is comparable to this.

1.23. Yama said: Choose sons and grandsons who shall live a hundred years; choose elephants, horses, herds of cattle and gold. Choose a vast empire on earth; live there as many years as you wish.

1.24. If you deem any other wish equal to that, choose it; choose wealth and a long life. Be the king, O Nachiketā, of the wide earth. I will make you the enjoyer of all desires.

1.25. Whatever desires are difficult to satisfy in this world of mortals, choose them as you wish: these fair maidens, with their chariots and musical instruments—men cannot obtain them. I give them to you and they shall wait upon you. But do not ask me about death.

1.26. Nachiketā said: But, O Death, **all these material enjoyments are very transient. Furthermore, they wear out the vigor of sense organs. Even the longest life is short indeed.** Keep your horses, dances and songs for yourself.

1.27. Man never gets satisfied with wealth. Moreover, since I have seen you, I shall certainly obtain wealth; I shall also live as long as you rule. But, no wish will be accepted by me other than

the one I have asked for.

1.28. Who among the mortals of the world—having reached the Imperishable—would rejoice a long life, after he has pondered over the temporary pleasures from beauty and song?

1.29. Tell me, O Death, of that supreme **life after death** about which a man has doubts. I do not choose any wish other than that incomprehensible one.

SECTION 2. EXISTENCE OF THE SUPREME BEING

Nachiketā passes the test

2.01. Yama said: The beneficial (श्रेयस) path is one thing and quite different is the path of sensual pleasures (प्रेयस). Both of these, serving different needs, bind a man. Blessed is he who chooses the beneficial path. He who chooses the path of sensual pleasures misses the goal of human life.

The path of Self-knowledge is beneficial and the path of material and sensual pleasure is harmful. Any desire is bondage. Thus both—the desire for sense pleasure and liberation—are bondages, although the latter is absolutely necessary as it ultimately relieves one from the bondage.

Sensual pleasures are, in fact, the source of misery in the end and have a beginning and an end. Therefore, the wise, O Arjuna, do not rejoice in sensual pleasures. **(BG** 5.22)

The pleasure that appears as poison in the beginning, but is like nectar in the end, comes by Self-knowledge and is in the mode of goodness. **(BG** 18.37) Sensual pleasures that appear as nectar in the beginning, but become poison in the end, are in the mode of passion. **(BG** 18.38)

The wise constantly reflect on the futility of sensual pleasures that inevitably become the cause of misery; therefore, they do not become victims of sensual cravings.

One who enjoys the ocean of the nectar of devotion has no use for the sensual pleasures that are like water of a pond. The river of material joy dries up quickly after the rainy season if there is no perennial source

of spiritual water. Material objects are like straws to the wise.

UPANISHADS

There is a path of joy and there is the path of pleasure. Pondering on them, the wise (one) chooses the of joy; the fool takes the path of pleasure.

2.02. Both the beneficial (श्रेयस) and the pleasant (प्रेयस) paths present themselves to a man. The calm soul, (in the mode of goodness) examines them well and prefers the beneficial over the pleasant; but the fool, (in the modes of passion and ignorance) chooses the pleasant out of greed and attachment.

2.03. O Nachiketā, after pondering well the pleasures that seem to be delightful, you have renounced them all. You have not taken **the road to wealth, where many men perish.**

2.04. Wide apart and leading to different ends are these two: the pleasant path of material and sensual enjoyment and the path of Knowledge. I regard you, O Nachiketā, an aspirant of Knowledge; for even many pleasures could not tempt you away.

2.05. Intellectuals dwelling in darkness—but thinking themselves to be wise—have to undergo many cycles of birth and death by following various difficult paths of rituals. Like a blind person led by a priest who is also blind, they miss the goal of human life.

Those who are dominated by material desires, consider the attainment of heaven as the highest goal of life. They engage in specific rites for the sake of material prosperity and enjoyment. Rebirth is the result of their action. **(BG** 2.43)

2.06. The Self never reveals itself to a person devoid of differentiation between the Real and the unreal, careless and perplexed by the delusion of wealth. "This world alone exists," he thinks, "and there is no other." Such a person comes under my control, again and again.

2.07. There are many who have not heard of Ātmā; though hearing of Him, many still do not understand. **It is rare to find the man who is able to teach the Self; and how blessed is he who comprehends the Self, when taught by an able Master.**

2.08. Ātmā can never be comprehended when taught by an inferior teacher, because it can be diversely explained and argued. But when it is taught by him who has become one with Ātmā, no more doubt remains. **Ātmā is subtler than the subtlest and not to be known by logic, but by sincere enquiry (Brahma-Jignāsā) and contemplation.**

2.09. This Knowledge cannot be obtained by reasoning. **Ātmā is easy to comprehend, O dearest, when taught by another awakened soul.** You have attained this Knowledge now. You are, indeed, a man of firm resolve. May we always get an inquirer like you!

The Requirement of Renunciation and Reflection

2.10. Yama said: I know that the fruit of action (such as Nachiketā sacrifice and other rituals) is not eternal; for **Eternal Self is never attained by non-eternal means.** Yet I have performed the Nachiketā sacrifice with the help of non-eternal means and attained this position which is only relatively eternal.

2.11. The fulfillment of desires, the foundation of the universe; and the fruits of sacrifice: freedom from fear of death and the wide heavenly pleasures—all these you have seen; and being wise you have rejected them with firm resolve.

2.12. The wise man gives up both joy and sorrow after having realized—by means of contemplation on the inner Self (ब्रह्मविचार)— that ancient, effulgent, un-manifest, hard to be seen (hidden by the veil of maya) and residing in the body.

2.13. The mortal—who has heard this and comprehended the subtle Self as the source of Dharma, who has differentiated Ātmā from body mind and all physical objects (निदिध्यासन)—rejoices, because he has obtained that which is the source of bliss, the Abode of Brahman. I believe the Supreme Abode is open for Nachiketā.

2.14. Nachiketā said: That which you know as beyond Dharma and Adharma, different from cause and effect, and different from past and future—tell me all about That.

Know Om as Brahman

2.15. Yama said: The goal which all the Vedas declare, which all austerities aim at, and which men desire when they lead the life of celibacy, I will tell you briefly: it is **Om!**

2.16. This mono-syllable Om is indeed Brahman. This syllable is the Highest. Whosoever knows this syllable obtains all that he desires.

2.17. Om is the best means of Self-realization; this is the highest method. Whosoever knows this Om is adored in the world of Brahman.

The Eternal Indestructible Soul

2.18. Know that the Spirit (Soul, Ātmā, Jivātmā or Jiva) is neither born nor does it ever die. It is not born from anything and nothing is born from it. It is birthless, eternal, everlasting and ancient, it is not destroyed when the body is destroyed.

The Spirit is neither born, nor does it die at any time. It does not come into being nor cease to exist. It is unborn, eternal, permanent, and primeval. The Spirit is not destroyed when the body is destroyed. **(BG 2.20)**

2.19. If the killer thinks he kills and if the killed thinks he is killed, neither of these has the right Knowledge. The Self neither kills, nor is killed.

One who thinks that the Spirit is a slayer, and one who thinks the Spirit is slain are both ignorant because the Spirit neither slays nor is slain. **(BG 2.19)**

Characteristics of the Supreme

2.20. Ātmā is smaller than the smallest and bigger than the biggest. It is hidden in the causal hearts of all living beings. A man who is free from desires beholds the majesty of the Self by equanimity of mind and senses and becomes free from all grief.

2.21. Though sitting still, it travels far; though lying down, it goes everywhere. Who, but advanced souls, can know that **luminous Ātmā who rejoices as a jiva and also does not rejoice as a witness? (Also see MuU 3.1.01 and ShU 4. 06)**

2.22. The wise one does not grieve, having known the bodiless, vast, immortal and all-pervading Ātmā dwelling in all mortal bodies.

Lord Krishna said: You grieve for those who are not worthy of grief and yet speak words of wisdom. The wise grieve neither for the living nor for the dead. **(BG** 2.11)

The Conditions for Knowing Brahman

2.23. Atman is not attained through discourses or through intellect or through much learning. It is gained by one who seeks it diligently (and qualifies for it). To such a person the Atman reveals its true nature. (The same as MuU 3.2.3)

This four-armed form of Mine that you have just seen cannot be seen even by study of the Vedas or by austerity or by acts of charity or by the performance of rituals. **(BG** 11.53) But by unswerving devotion (or Knowledge), I can be seen in this form, can be known in essence, and also can be reached, O Arjuna. **(BG** 11.54)

2.24. Neither those who have not turned away from wickedness, nor the unrestrained or the un-meditative, nor the one whose mind is not at peace, can attain this even by Knowledge.

God is called the All Mighty!

2.25. He to whom the good and mighty people such as the Brāhmanas and the Kshatriyas classes are (as it were) but food, and the lord of Death a condiment (chatani चटनी), how can one know where He is? *(Thus Self or God is the mightiest of the mighty and is called the All Mighty!)*

SECTION 3. SĀDHANĀ

The Universal and Individual Soul

3.01. Two beings (jivātmā and Paramātmā) dwell within the body, in the intellect and in the supreme space of the causal heart. Jivātmā tastes the fruits of his own deeds. The knowers of Brahman—as well as well as those householders who have offered oblations in the Five Fires and also those who have performed the Nachiketā fire sacrifice three times—describe Paramātmā as the light and jivātmā as the shadow or reflection of the light.

Nachiketā Sacrificial Fire as an Aid

3.02. We know how to perform the Nachiketā sacrifice, which is the **bridge to heaven** for sacrificers. We also know the Supreme, imperishable Brahman, which is sought by those who wish to cross over to the spiritual shore where there is no fear of death.

Homeward Journey of the jiva in a Chariot

HOW TO CONTROL LUST AND REACH THE GOAL
Also read: www.gita-society.com/bhagavad-gita.html#journey

3.03. Know that the Paramātmā is the owner of the chariot, Jivātmā or jiva is the passenger in the chariot; the body is the chariot; the intellect is the charioteer; and a well-controlled mind is the rein.

3.04. The senses, they say, are the horses; the sense objects, the roads. The wise call Lord the enjoyer, when He is united with the body, the senses and the mind by becoming a jiva.

3.05. If one is of unrestrained mind, devoid of differentiation between the Real and the unreal, his senses become uncontrollable, like the wicked horses of a charioteer.

3.06. But one who has control over the mind and possesses differentiation between the Real and the unreal, then the senses come under control, like the trained horses of a charioteer.

Note 3: The mind is the rein to control the senses, but mind itself has to be reined by a strong intellect. Only a controlled mind can control the sense-horses as mentioned below:

Control of the mind is Necessary

3.**07.** One who is devoid of Knowledge, thoughtless and impure never attains the goal, but enters into the rounds of birth and death.

3.08. But one who is intelligent, pure and has control over his mind, verily reaches the goal and is not born again.

3.09. A man who has a purified (or strong) intellect as his charioteer and a well-controlled mind—he reaches the goal, the Supreme abode of Vishnu.

Order of Progression to the Supreme

3.**10–11. Superior to the senses are the sense objects; superior to the sense objects is the mind; superior to the mind, the intellect; superior to the intellect is Knowledge, superior to Knowledge is Brahman; superior to Brahman is the ParaBrahman (Purusha or the Absolute). Beyond the Absolute there is nothing: this is the end, the Supreme Goal.**

(Also see KaU 6.07-08, MB 12.204.10, and BG 3.42)

The Method of Yoga

3.12. That Self hidden inside all beings does not reveal itself to all. It is seen only by the seers through their one-pointed and sharp intellect.

3.13. The wise man should drown his speech in his mind and his mind in his intellect and his intellect in the Cosmic Mind and the Cosmic Mind in the Universal Self.

Here reference seem to be the yogic practice of samyama (concentration (धारणा), reflection (ध्यान) and trance (समाधि)) to submerge the mind in the Self.

A call to the Way of Liberation from Death

3.14. Arise! Awake! Approach a sad-guru and learn. Like the sharp edge of a sword is that path to God, so the wise say: Hard to walk and difficult to cross and reach the goal.

The path of spiritual life is very slippery and has to be trodden very carefully to avoid falls. It is not a joyous ferryboat ride, but a very difficult path. It is like treading on the sharp edge of a sword.

3.15. Having realized Ātmā as soundless, intangible, formless, imperishable, tasteless, eternal, odorless, without beginning or end and unchanging—one is freed from the jaws of Death.

The Immortal Value of this Teaching

3.16. The wise one having heard and imparted this ancient story of Nachiketā, as told by the lord of Death, to others is glorified in the world of Brahman.

3.17. And he who, practicing self-control, recites this supreme secret in an assembly of devotees or at an after-death ceremony (Shrāddha) obtains immortality.

SECTION 4. THE INNER WAY OF THE SPIRIT

The Self cannot be Sought Through the Senses

4.01. Yama said: The self-existent Supreme has made the senses such that they go outward, and hence man sees the external objects only and not the internal Self. But a wise man with his senses averted from sense-objects and desirous of immortality, beholds the Self within.

4.02. The ignorant pursue sensual pleasures and fall into the net of wide spread transmigration. But the wise, having known the immortal amidst all mortals, do not desire anything in this world.

Ātmā is working in All the Senses, in All states

4.03. Through Ātmā one sees, knows, tastes, smells, hears, touches and enjoys sensual pleasures. Is there anything that remains unknown to Ātmā? This is That knower you wanted to know.

4.04. It is through Ātmā that one perceives all objects in waking and dream states. Having known the vast, all-pervading Ātmā, the wise does not grieve.

Universal Soul is same as the Individual Soul

4.05. He who knows this Ātmā as the enjoyer of the fruits of action by becoming jiva, the sustainer of life and the Lord of the past, present and the future, and as very near (within the body)—he has no fear of death.

4.06. He who knows that Brahman came first before creation began and dwells inside the body made up of the five basic elements (earth, water, fire, air, and the subtle Ethereal substance, Ākāsha), actually knows Brahman. This is verily That.

4.07. The soul of gods (Brahmā)—who manifested in the form of Prāna with its five major components—enters the body and abides in the cavity of the causal heart. One who knows this knows Brahman, indeed. This is verily That.

4.08. Agni, hidden in the wood-sticks and well-guarded—like a child in the womb by its mother—is worshipped day after day by wise men and by those who offer oblations in the sacrifices. This is verily That.

4.09. That from which the universe comes out and into which it merges again, on which all Devas depend, and no one can ever surpass. This is indeed That.

The Cause of Rebirth

4.10. What is here, the same is there and what is there, the same is here. He goes from death to death who sees any difference between Brahman and the world.

The wise see no difference between the microcosm (व्यष्टि) and macrocosm (समष्टि). This is a very important key verse.

4.11. By the mind and intellect alone Brahman is realized; then one does not see any difference, whatsoever, between the creator and the creation. He goes from death to death who sees any difference between the creator and the creation.

The Eternal Lord Abides In One's Body

4.12. The Purusha, the size of a thumb, dwells in the body. He is the Lord of the past, present and the future. After knowing Him, one does not have any fear of death. This is indeed Brahman.

4.13. The Purusha, the size of a thumb, is like a bright white flame of the lamp without smoke. The Lord of the past, present and the future, is the same today and tomorrow. This is indeed Brahman.

The Results of Seeing Diversity in Unity

4.14. As the rainwater falling on a mountain top, when distracted by some external forces, runs down the slope in all directions and does not reach the ocean; similarly, **those who see the creation as different from the Creator, verily run after the distractions of creation (or maya) and do not reach the goal of human birth.**

4.15. As pure water poured into pure water becomes one with it, so also, O Nachiketā, does the pure soul of the sage who knows becomes one with the Self. (An impure soul cannot merge in pure Brahman).

SECTION 5. THE STAGES OF SELF-CONTROL

The Individual soul and the creation

5.01. There is a city with nine gates belonging to Ātmā as His residence. He who meditates on Him as such grieves no more; liberated from the bonds of ignorance, becomes free. This is indeed Brahman.

The human body has been called the City of Nine Gates (or openings) in the scriptures. The nine openings are: Two openings each for the eyes, ears, and nose; and one each for the mouth, anus, and urethra. The Lord of all beings and the universe resides in this city with the individual soul (Jiva) performing and directing all action. (Also see **BG 13.**22)

A person, who has completely renounced the attachment to the fruits of all work from his mind, dwells happily in the City of Nine Gates, neither performing nor directing action. (**BG** 5.13)

5.02. He is the sun dwelling in the sky. He is the air in the sky. He is the fire. He is the guest dwelling in the house. He dwells in men, in the gods, in truth, in the space. He is born in the water, on earth and as a river on the mountains. He is the Truth (Knowledge) and He is Great.

5.03. He is the One who sends Prāna upward and leads Apāna downward. All Devas (gods) worship that adorable One seated in the causal heart.

5.04. When the soul—the owner of the body and dwelling in it as jiva—is separated from the body after death and is freed from the body, what remains are the five basic elements. This is, verily, That.

5.05. No mortal ever lives by Prāna alone, which goes up, nor by Apāna, which goes down. Men live by the Spirit of Brahman on which Prāna and Apāna also depend.

Embodiment of the Reincarnating Soul

5.06. Well then, Nachiketā, I shall tell you again about this mysterious eternal Brahman and also about what happens to the Ātmā after meeting death.

5.07. Some souls enter the womb to have another human body, others go to animals, plants and insects according to their Karma and Knowledge.

(Read more in the Gita Chapter 14 verses: 14, 15, 18 and 19)

One's Real Self is the Same as the Universal Self

5.08. He, the Purusha, who remains active and a witness while the sense-organs are asleep or shaping one lovely form after another in a dream world, that indeed is Brahman and that alone is called the immortal. All worlds are contained in Him and none can outshine Him. This, indeed, is Brahman.

5.09. As one fire, after entering the world of woods, assumes different forms according to the type of wood it enters, similarly one Ātman that exists in all beings appears different according to the forms of the objects it enters. It also exists outside all forms in its original transcendental form.

5.10. As one air (or water) after it enters an object, assumes different forms according to the different objects it enters, similarly the one Ātman that exists in all being appears to have different forms according to the objects it enters. It also exists outside all forms in its original transcendental form.

5.11. As the sun, the Eye of the whole world, is not affected by the blemishes of the eyes or by the objects lighted by the sun, similarly the one Ātmā, dwelling in all beings, is un-affected by the miseries of the world, being beyond the world. *(Just as the rope is not affected by the appearance of snake-in-the rope.)*

Indescribable Bliss of Self-Realization

5.12. There is only one Supreme Ruler, the inmost Self of all beings, who makes His one form manifold. Eternal happiness belongs to the wise—who perceive Him within themselves—and not to others.

5.13. There is One eternal Reality among non-eternal objects, the consciousness in the conscious objects and who, though One, fulfils the desires of many. **Eternal peace belongs to the wise—who perceive Him within themselves—and not to others.**

5.14. The sages realize that indescribable Supreme Joy as "This is That." How shall I know That? Is it self-luminous or does it shine by another's light? The answer comes:

The Self-Luminous Light of the World

5.15. The sun does not illumine Him, nor the moon and the stars, nor these lightning or the fire. Everything (sun, moon, stars, lightning, fire etc.) shines by His energy (or light, power). By His light all this is lighted.

The Supreme Abode is self-luminous, not illumined by any other source. He illumines the sun and the moon as a luminous lamp illumines other objects. Similar verses appear in other Upanishads (See MuU 2.2.10, ShU 6.14) and the Bhagavad-Gita:

The sun does not illumine My Supreme Abode, nor does the moon, nor the fire. Having reached there, people attain permanent liberation (Moksha) and do not come back to this temporal world. (BG 15.06) The light energy of the sun which illumines the entire world, which is in the moon and in the fire, know that light to be Mine. (BG 15.12).

Abode of the Supreme Being is self-luminous, not illumined by any other source. He illumines the sun and the moon as a luminous lamp illumines other objects. Transcendental light of Brahman (Divine Light, Brahma Jyoti) is the source of all light energy and is called the light of all lights in **BG** 13.17. The Supreme Being existed before the sun, moon, and fire came into existence during creation, and it will exist even after everything gets dissolved into unmanifest Nature during complete dissolution. The word 'light' has also been symbolically used to indicate the light of Knowledge.

SECTION 6. THE TREE OF LIFE

Brahman is the source of the Cosmos

6.01. This cosmos is like an eternal Ashvattha tree with its root above (in Brahman) and branches (Cosmos) below. That Brahman is bright. That is Brahman and That alone exists and is immortal. In Brahman all worlds are contained and nothing is beyond That. This is indeed Brahman (Also see **BG** 15.01)

The Great Fear of Brahman

6.02. This whole universe evolved from it and is supported by Brahman's energy, the Prāna. Brahman is very stern and a just controller with a thunderbolt. **No one can escape from His laws.** Those who thus know It become immortal.

6.03. From fear of Brahman, fire burns, the sun shines, Indra, Vāyu and the fifth: the lord of Death perform their respective duties.

Degrees of Perception of the Self

6.04. If a man is able to comprehend or know Brahman before death, he is liberated; if not, one has to take birth again and again in the created worlds.

6.05. On the earth, Brahman can be very clearly seen—as in a mirror—in one's own inner psyche. In the World of the forefathers (pitriLoka, manes), it can be seen like one sees objects in dream; In the world of the Gandharvas, it is seen like one sees an image in water; and in the abode of Brahmā, it is seen as light and shade.

The Gradation Up To the Cosmic Being

6.06. Having known that the senses have their separate origin from Prakriti and they are distinct from Ātmā and also that their actions belong to senses alone and not to Ātmā, a wise man is no more bothered by sense objects.

6.07. Superior to the senses is the mind, superior to the mind is the intellect, higher than the intellect is the avyakta (or the unmanifest) Brahman, higher than unmanifest Brahman is the Brahman.

6.08. Superior to the Brahman is the all-pervading and imperceptible **Supreme Being—Paramātmā, the highest Absolute.** Having realized Him, the embodied soul becomes liberated and attains immortality.

The senses are said to be superior to the body; superior to senses are the sense objects; superior to sense objects is the mind; superior to mind is the intellect; superior to intellect is the Self-Knowledge; and the Self is the highest. **(BG** 3.42)

Thus, knowing (your true nature as) the Self to be the highest, and controlling the mind by the intellect (that is purified and made strong by Self-knowledge), one must kill this mighty enemy, lust (with the sword of true Knowledge of the Self), O Arjuna. **(BG** 3.43)

6.09. His transcendental form is not within the field of our vision; none can see Him with the physical eyes. One can know Him when He is revealed by the intuition of purified intellect that is free from all doubts; and by constant contemplation (आत्म-विचार). **Those who know Him become immortal** (य एतद् विदुरऽमृतास्ते भवन्ति).

The Method of Yoga

6.10. When the five senses of perception lie still, together with the mind; and when the intellect does not work, that is the Supreme or Super-conscious state of mind.

6.11. The firm Control of the mind and senses (स्थिराम् इन्द्रिय धारणाम्) is called yoga. Then the yogi becomes free from the erratic behavior of mind. **But, one must be very vigilant, for the yoga can be acquired only with great difficulty and lost easily (but Knowledge can never be lost!).**

The Self is attained by faith in Scriptures

6.12. Ātmā can never be reached by mind nor speech, nor by eyes. **It is only realized by faith in the words of sages who have realized it and say: He exists. (Also see BG 13.25)**

6.13. He is to be realized first in manifest aspect (साकार रूप), and then in His true transcendental, un-manifest aspect (निराकार रूप). Of these two aspects, Ātmā realized as manifest leads the knower to the realization of His true un-manifest aspect. (Also see IsU 14)

Requires Renunciation of Desires, Attachments

6.14. When all the desires that dwell in the heart go away at the dawn of Knowledge, then the mortal becomes immortal and immediately attains Brahman.

By transcendental Knowledge one truly understands what and who I am in essence. Having known Me in essence, one immediately becomes one with Me. **(BG** 18.55)

6.15. When all the ties (desires, attachments, ego etc.) are severed by Knowledge, then the mortal becomes immortal— in this body on the earth. This alone is the summary of all the Vedāntic teachings.

6.16. There are one hundred and one arteries (nādis) of the heart, only one of them—the Sushumnā nādi—pierces the crown of the head. Going upward by it, a man at death attains immortality. But when his Prāna passes out by any other arteries, one is reborn in the world.

6.17. The Spirit, not larger than a thumb, is always seated in the causal heart of all beings. One should distinguish Spirit from the body as one distinguishes grain from the husk. One must know that the Self (or Spirit) is pure and immortal.

This Teaching: A Way to Immortality

6.18. Having received this wisdom taught by the King of Death and the entire process of yoga, Nachiketā became free from impurities and fear of death (अभिनिवेश) and attained Brahman. Thus, it will be also with any other who knows the inner Self in this manner.

OM TAT SAT

4. PRASHNA UPANISHAD

The Prashna Upanishad or **PrashnoPanishad** is one of the earlier, primary Upanishads. It is associated with the Atharvaveda. It has 67 verses written in prose. Rishi Pippalāda answers six questions: (1) matter (rayi) and energy (Prāna) is the origin of creation, (2) Prāna is the power of God, (3) God is the origin of Prāna, (4) the three states of consciousness, (5) meditation on Om, and (6) Ātmā resides as Prāna in the body.

QUESTION 1. THE ORIGIN OF CREATION

1.01. Om! Six students, devoted to Brahman and seeking the Supreme Brahman, approached the venerable rishi (sage) Pippalāda with a gift of fuel-wood in hand thinking that he would tell them everything about Brahman.

1.02. The rishi Pippalāda said to them: Stay with me a year practicing austerities, chastity and faith. Then you may ask questions according to your desires. If I know them I shall tell you everything.

1.03. Then Kabandhi, the son of Katya, came to him after a year and asked: Sir, where are these creatures born from?

1.04. To him the teacher said: Prajāpati (Brahmā), the Lord of Creatures, was desirous of progeny. **He performed austerities (तपस) and having performed austerities, created the pair: matter (Rayi) and energy (Prāna). He said to Himself: "This pair will produce creatures for Me in manifold ways."**

'Austerity' here means samkalpa or Divine Will to create: "**Eko'ham bahu syām (Let Me be many, ChU 6.2.3)**". In Brahman, there is the thought vibration of **Om** and the universe is projected out of Him. He entered into every being just as a huge fig (banyan) tree is projected out of a tiny seed and the seed remains in every fig.

1.05. The Sun is Prāna, the energy that supports life; the Moon is Rayi or primordial matter (Adi Prakriti). Matter is, indeed, all this—what has form and what is formless. Therefore everything having form is, indeed, matter (Moon, Rayi).

1.06. The sun, when it rises, enters the eastern quarter and thereby holds the living beings of the east by its rays. When it illumines the southern, western, northern, lower, upper and the intermediate quarters (or directions)—it illumines everything and supports all living beings by its rays.

1.07-08. The sun is the soul of all forms, it is life. It is Prāna, the heat energy that rises everyday. The wise know him who is in all forms, full of rays, all-knowing, non-dual, the eye of all beings, the giver of heat. The sun rises with thousands of rays that support the life of all creatures.

1.09. The year, verily, is Prajāpati (Lord of the creatures) and his paths are two: the Southern and the Northern. Those who perform sacrifices and engage in pious actions, go to the World of the Moon (heaven) by the Southern path; verily they return to earth again. Therefore, the rishis who desire off-spring travel by the Southern Path.

1.10. But those who seek the Self through austerity, chastity, faith and Knowledge travel by the Northern Path and attain SunLoka, from where they do not return back to earth. This path is blocked for the ignorant.

1.11. Some call Sun the father with twelve forms (months), the giver of rain and the dweller in the region above the sky. Others, say that the Sun is omniscient, placed on a chariot with seven wheels (seven colors of the rainbow) and six spokes or seasons.

(The word "Sun or sun" has been also used for the Supreme Being)

1.12. The month is Prajāpati. Its dark fortnight is matter, rayi; its bright half, the eater, Prāna. Therefore some rishis perform sacrifice in the bright half, some in the other half of the lunar month.

1.13. Day and night are Prajāpati. Day is Prāna (energy) and night is the matter or Rayi. Those who join in sexual enjoyment during day dissipate their Prāna more; but to join in sexual enjoyment by night is said to have self-control or celibacy by some.

1.14. Food is Prajāpati. From food comes semen; from semen all creatures are born.

1.15. Those who follow the rule of Prajāpati should produce a pair of children, a son and a daughter. But Brahmā-loka belongs to those who observe austerity and chastity and are firmly established in Knowledge.

1.16. The pure world of Brahmā belongs only to those in whom there is no deceit, falsehood or deception.

QUESTION 2. PRĀNA IS GOD

2.01. Then Vaidarbhi, belonging to the family of Bhrigu, asked him: Sir, how many gods support the body of the created being? How many of them manifest their power? And which one of them is the greatest?

2.02. To the disciple he said: Ākāsha (ether, the origin of the other four basic elements), verily is that God; together with the air, fire, water, earth together with the speech, mind, eye and ear. These, having manifested their power, said boastfully: "We support this body and uphold it."

2.03. To them the chief Prāna said: "Do not fall into delusion. I, the Universal life force alone, dividing myself into five vital breaths [Prāna (inhalation), apāna (exhalation, excretion), samāna (digestive fire), udāna (speech) and vyāna (blood circulation)] support this body and uphold it." The other gods were not convinced.

2.04. Prāna, out of pride, rose upward from the body. Now, when it rose upward all the others rose upward also and when it settled down they all settled down with it. As bees go out when their queen goes out and return when she returns, even so did speech, mind, eye and ear. They were now satisfied and praised Prāna.

2.05. Prāna burns as fire. It is the sun, the rain, the rain god, the wind, the earth, it is food. It is the luminous god. It is the visible and the invisible; it is the basis of (relative) immortality of even gods.

2.06. Like spokes in the hub of a wheel, all are fixed in Prāna, including the birth of Rigveda, the Yajurveda, the Sāmaveda, the Kshatriyas, the Brāhmans and all beings.

2.07. As Prajāpati, the universal life force, you (Prāna) move about in the womb; it is you, indeed, who are born again. O Prāna, creatures bring offerings to you, who dwell in the body and in the organs.

2.08. You are the chief carrier of oblations to the gods and the offering to the departed fathers; you are the senses of the rishis.

2.09. You are the creator, the supporter and the destroyer too. You move in the sky as the sun-god, the lord of lights.

2.10. O Prāna, when you shower down rain, these creatures of yours are delighted, thinking there will be as much food as they desire.

2.11. O Prāna, You are pure. You are the Fire that enjoys the offerings by the devotees. You are the Supreme Lord of all. We are the givers of oblations that you consume. You are our father.

2.12. These forms of yours—which abide in speech, which abide in the ear, which abide in the eye and which pervade the mind—make it stay and auspicious.

2.13. Whatever exists in the three worlds is all under the control of Prāna. O Prāna, protect us as a mother protects her sons; give us prosperity and wisdom.

QUESTION 3. THE ORIGIN OF PRĀNA

3.01. Then Kausalya, the son of Asvala, asked Pippalāda: Sir, Where is this Prāna born from? How does it come and abide in the body of all? How does it depart from body? How does it support the external world and the internal world (all the six senses)?

3.02. To him the teacher replied: You are asking such difficult questions; you must be exceedingly devoted to Brahman. Therefore I will answer you.

3.03. This Prāna or energy is born of Ātman. As a shadow is cast by a person, so this Prāna is cast by Ātman. It is the action of the mind that causes Prāna to enter into the body.

3.04. As an emperor commands his officials, saying: "Reside here and rule those villages," so this chief of Prāna engages the other five major Prānas in their different functions,

3.05. Apāna dwells in the organs of excretion and procreation; Prāna himself moves through these four organs: the mouth, the nose, the eye and the ear. In the middle of the body dwells samāna; it distributes what has been offered as food in the stomach to all parts of the body.

3.06. The Ātman dwells in the causal heart, where there are one hundred and one arteries (nādis); for each of these there are one hundred veins or branches and for each of these veins, again, there are seventy-two thousand subsidiary veins. Vyāna circulates blood in all these 101x100x72,000=727,200,000 total branches.

3.07. And then udāna, ascending upward to the crown in the head, through sushumnā nādi, takes the departing soul to the virtuous world of heaven for its virtuous deeds; and to the sinful world of animals, insects and plants for its sinful deeds; and to the world of humans, for mixed deeds.

3.08. The rays of the sun are the cosmic Prāna in the eye that make the eye see. The deity (gravity) that exists in the earth attracts the apāna towards earth. The space or ākāsha between the heaven and the earth is samāna. The air is vyāna.

3.09. The internal fire (body temperature) is udāna; therefore those in whom this fire has been extinguished die, taking the senses with the subtle body.

The jiva takes its subtle body—the six sensory faculties of perception, mind, intellect, ego, and five vital forces (Prāna)—from one physical body to another after death, just as the wind carries away aroma from the flower **(BG** 15.08).

3.10. Whatever one's thought, with that one enters into Prāna. Prāna united with udāna leads Jivātmā to whatever world has been created by the predominant thought during one's life-time.

Whatever object one remembers as one leaves the body at the end of life, that object is attained. Thought of whatever object prevails during one's lifetime, one remembers only that object at the end of life and achieves it. (**BG** 8.06)

One's destiny is determined by the predominant thought at the time of death. Even if one has practiced devotion and God-consciousness during one's lifetime, the thought of God may or may not come at the hour of death. Therefore, God-consciousness should be continued till death.

3.11. The wise one who knows Prāna as described above attains immortality and his Knowledge does not perish.

3.12. He who knows the origin of Prāna, its entry, its place, its fivefold distribution, its all-pervasive internal and external aspects as described above, obtains immortality in the space of Brahmā (Brahmā-loka) until the end of the creative cycle for sure.

QUESTION 4. THREE STATES OF CONSCIOUSNESS

4.01. Next Sauryayāni, belonging to the family of Garga, asked: Sir, what is it that sleeps in man and becomes awake again? Which deity is it that sees dreams? Who enjoys and remembers the bliss of a deep sleep? In whom do all these senses and organs abide during sleep?

4.02. To him Pippalāda replied: O Gargya, as the rays of the setting sun remain dormant in the luminous orb and again come out when sun rises, similarly, all these—the sense objects and the senses together with the mind—take rest. Therefore, during deep sleep (सुषुप्ति) a man does not hear, see, smell, taste, touch, speak, grasp, enjoy, secrete and does not move.

4.03. The Prāna alone remains awake or active in the body of a sleeping man. The Prāna(s) are also called by other names.

4.04. Samāna is so called because it carries the out-breathing and the in-breathing equally (Samāna) into the body. Thus, Samāna is the priest. The mind is the sacrificer. Udāna is the fruit of the sacrifice, because it takes the sacrificer, the mind, **close to Brahman** every day during deep sleep.

4.05. In dream state the mind experiences the Glory of God. Whatever has been seen it sees again; whatever has been heard it hears again; whatever has been experienced in different places at different times, it experiences again. Whatever has been seen or not seen, heard or not heard and whatever is real or not real—the mind sees it all. The mind itself becomes the dreamer as well as all the objects of the dream world. *(Similarly, Creator itself becomes the Creation!)*

4.06. When the mind is subdued by that unknown power causing the deep sleep (सुषुप्ति), jiva sees no dream; at that time, in this body, temporary bliss is enjoyed by the mind.

4.07-08. just as birds go to a tree to rest, so do all the following rest in the Supreme Ātman: The earth and its subtle elements, water and its subtle elements, fire and its subtle elements, air and its subtle elements, ākāsha and its subtle elements, the eye and what can be seen, the ear and what can be heard, the nose and what can be smelt, the taste and what can be tasted, the skin and what can be touched, the organ of speech and what can be spoken, the hands and what can be grasped, the organ of generation and what can be enjoyed, the organ of excretion and what can be excreted, the feet and what is their destination, the mind and what can be thought, the intellect and what can be comprehended, the ego and the object of egoism, the memory and its object, knowledge and its object, Prāna and everything supported by it—all these rest in Ātman during deep sleep.

4.09. It is He who sees, feels, hears, smells, tastes, thinks and knows. He is the doer, the ego, the Purusha. Becoming a jiva, He dwells in the imperishable Self.

4.10. One who knows that imperishable Being is bright, without shadow, without body and without color—verily attains the Supreme. O my good friend, **one who knows Ātman, becomes all-knowing and becomes all.**

4.11. He, O friend, who knows that imperishable Being—in which rest the mind, the intellect, the senses, the ego, the gods, the Prānas, the five elements and all—becomes omniscient (all-knowing) and realizing himSelf as Ātman, feels himself as infinite Self—existing everywhere and in all. Such a person is called Self-realized or ParamaHamsa.

There is nothing other than Me, the Supreme Being, O Arjuna. Everything in the universe rests in Me like different thread-beads rest on the thread. **(BG** 7.07)

QUESTION 5. MEDITATION ON OM

5.01. Then Satyakāma, the son of Sibi, asked Pippalāda: Sir, to what world does one go to who regularly meditates on **Om**?

5.02. He replied: O Satyakāma, the syllable Om is the symbol of both the ParaBrahman and Brahman and also the other Brahman (gods). Therefore, he who thus knows Om, the all comprehensive sound-symbol of Brahman, surely attains one of them, depending on the degree of one's understanding.

5.03. If he meditates on one letter A; becoming enlightened by that alone, he quickly comes back to earth after death. The rik deva leads him to the world of men. By practicing austerity, chastity and faith he attains greatness on the earth.

5.04. If, again, he meditates on the second letter U, he is led up by the mantra deity of yajur verses to the world of moon or heaven. He returns to this world after enjoying greatness in the heaven.

5.05. Again, he who meditates on the Supreme through the mono-syllable Om, becomes united with the Sun (the light of Knowledge). He is freed from all sin just like a snake is freed from its old skin. He is taken to the world of Brahmā by Sāma hymns via Northern path—the path of gods. Once there he attains gradual liberation (KramaMukti).

5.06. When the three letters of AUM are meditated upon separately (like A.... U.... M), the contemplator is born again and again; but when they are meditated together as **Om**, it is said to be meditated properly on all the activities of the three states—waking, dream and sleep—of consciousness; one does not waver from Brahma-consciousness (आत्मभाव).

5.07. The wise man, meditating on letter A, attains this world by means of the rik verses; attains heaven by means of the yajur verses (by meditating on letter U); and obtains Knowledge by means of the sāma verses (by meditating on Om). It is through the mono-syllable **Om** that one realizes what is tranquil, immortal, and becomes free from fear of death. This is the Highest.

(Learn a proper technique of meditation on **Om** on pages 58-60)

QUESTION 6. THE ABODE OF ĀTMĀ

6.01. Then Sukesa, the son of Bhāradvāja, said to Pippalāda: Sir, Hiranyabha, the prince of Kosala, once came to me and asked this question: "O son of Bhāradvāja, do you know the person with sixteen Kalā or parts?" I said to the prince: "I do not know Him; if I knew Him, why should I not tell you? Surely he who speaks what is not true withers away to the very root; therefore I should not speak untruth." Then he silently mounted his chariot and went away. Now I ask you: Where does that Person dwell?

Sixteen components (Kalā, parts) of the Supreme

6.02. Pippalāda said to him: My dear friend, the Supreme Person (purusha)—from whom these sixteen parts arise— dwells here, within this body and in the entire creation.

6.03. The Purusha reflected: "What is it by whose departure I shall depart and by whose staying I shall stay in the creation?"

6.04. Thus, He created Prāna; from Prāna Ākāsha, air, fire, water, earth, the organs, mind, intellect and matter; from matter (or food) vigor, austerity, mantra, karma and the universe; and in the universe He created different forms with names.

Thus, Prāna is the basis of all other fifteen parts mentioned above.

6.05. When ocean bound rivers reach the sea, their names and forms disappear and are called simply the ocean. Similarly these sixteen parts disappear when they turn inward towards their Real source, and away from the false identification with the parts. The parts then become one with the whole—the immortal Brahman.

6.06. Know that Purusha—who alone is to be known and in whom the parts rest like the spokes in the center of a wheel—so that death may not affect you.

6.07. Sage Pippalāda said to them: As far as I know, there is nothing higher than the ParaBrahman.

6.08. The students worshipping him said: You, indeed, are our father—you have taken us across our ocean of ignorance to the spiritual shore of Knowledge. Adoration to the supreme rishis! Adoration to the supreme rishis!

OM TAT SAT

The wise see God in all and all in God

5. MUNDAKA UPANISHAD

The **Mundaka Upanishad** is one of the earlier, primary Upanishads associated with the Atharvaveda. It has **64 verses in poetry**. This Upanishad discusses the purpose of creation, the purpose of rituals and its futility, Knowledge of Brahman, metaphor of bow, arrow and the target, analogy of two birds and how to attain Brahman.

CHAPTER 1. Section 1

1.1.01. Om! Brahmā, the Maker of the universe and the Preserver of the world, was the first among devas. He told His eldest son Atharvā about the Knowledge of Brahman, the foundation of all Knowledge.

1.1.02. The Knowledge of Brahman was first taught by Brahmā to Atharvā, Atharvā taught to Angira. Angira taught it to Satyavāhā, belonging to the clan of Bhāradvāja, and the latter taught it, in succession, to Angiras

1.1.03. Saunaka, the great householder, approached Angiras in the proper manner and said: Sir, what is that by knowing which everything in the universe becomes known?

The same question was also posed by Lord Krishna in the Bhagavad-Gita when He said to Arjuna:

I shall impart to you both the transcendental Knowledge and the transcendental experience or a vision, after knowing that nothing more remains to be known in this world. **(BG** 7.02)

When one firmly knows that everything in this universe is Brahman, then he knows everything as Brahman and nothing else. Thus everything becomes known to a Self-realized soul as "Brahman" only and nothing else!

Two types of knowledge

1.1.04. To him he said: Two types of knowledge must be known—that is what the knowers of Brahman tell us. They are the Higher Knowledge and the lower knowledge.

1.1.05. Of these two, the lower knowledge is the Rig-Veda, the Yajurveda, the Sāmaveda, and the Atharvaveda. Six auxiliary disciplines of the Vedas (called Vedānga) associated with study of the Vedas are: siksha (rules for correct pronunciation), kalpa (details of rituals), vyākaranam (grammar), nirukta (etymology, explanation of difficult words), chhandas (prosody), and jyotish (astronomy). The Higher Knowledge is that by which Brahman is attained.

1.1.06. By means of the Higher Knowledge the wise see Brahman everywhere and in everything; otherwise Brahman cannot be seen or grasped, because He has no attributes, no eyes or ears, no hands or feet. He is eternal and omnipresent, all-pervading and extremely subtle. He is imperishable and the source of all beings.

The theory and purpose of creation

1.1.07. As the spider sends forth and draws in its thread, as plants grow on the earth, as hair grows on the head and the body of a living man—so does everything in the universe *naturally arise* from the Imperishable.

Creation is a natural effortless projection of the powers of Spirit and is therefore purposeless. **The creative activity of the Lord is a mere pastime of the divine power (maya) without any purpose or motive.** It is nothing but an apparent natural modification of His infinite limitless energy (E) into matter (m) and vice versa (E=mc^2 of **Einstein**) done as His mere pastime. (Also see ShU 4.01)

1.1.08. Brahman creates the universe by Tapas[1] (तपस)—decision (samkalpa) or His Will to create. From His primal **Energy,** primal matter, Annam[2], is produced; and from primal matter, the Prāna, the mind, the five elements, the worlds, the works and the fruits of works: one after another.

[1] Tapas implies both heat and thought. Maxmuller translates it as 'brooding' of Brahman. This is the same as Brahma-samkalpa. It generally means deep thinking on Brahman (ब्रह्म-विचार, आत्म चिन्तन). Deep concentration of mind is called the highest tapas in **MB 12.250.04.**

[2] The word **'annam'** is used here not for the food we eat, but the primal matter out of which material objects, including food, are made by God.

1.1.09. From Brahman—who knows all and understands everything, whose creative power is Knowledge itself—is born Brahmā (the creative force); then came name, form, and food.

Section 2

1.2.01. This is the Truth: The ritualistic works which were revealed to the rishis in the hymns, have been described in many ways in the three Vedas. Perform them, being desirous to enjoy their fruits. This is your path leading to heaven.

1.2.02. When the fire is well lit and the flames begin to move, one can then offer his oblations—in the space between the two portions of the fire—by pouring clarified butter (Ghee).

1.2.03. When the Agnihotra sacrifice is not regularly performed at the full moon, new moon, the four months of autumn, and during the harvest time, at the right time, without guests, worship, feeding of animals, birds and trees; or is it is performed contrary to injunctions of the Vedas—then he cannot attain any of the seven worlds (bhur, bhuvar, svar, mahar, jana, tapas and satya).

1.2.04. The seven types of flames are: black, fierce, swift as mind, deep red, smoke colored, sparkling, and shining.

1.2.05. When the sacrificial oblations are offered at the proper time into these shining flames, his oblations are carried by the flames and the rays of the sun to heaven where the King of gods, Indra, dwells.

Rituals lead to Heaven

1.2.06. These bright oblations await the sacrificer and remain ready to greet him in the heaven by such words: "Welcome, welcome!! This is the world of heaven gained by your good deeds!"

After describing the almost impossible task of performing rituals correctly, in a great detail, the wise rishi now gives a stern warning by pointing out the utter futility, in attainment of the goal of human life, to all those who are attached to such rituals.

1.2.07. Verily, frail indeed are those rafts of sacrifices, conducted by eighteen persons (sixteen priests plus the sacrificer and his wife), upon whom rests such inferior spiritual practice. **Fools who rejoice in them as the Highest Goal, fall victims again and again to old age and death.**

The resolute determination for God-realization is not possible for those ignorant ones who are attached to pleasure and power and whose judgment is obscured by ritualistic activities for fulfillment of material desires. **(BG** 2.44)

1.2.08. Fools—dwelling in darkness, yet thinking themselves to be wise and learned, puffed up with vain scholarship—go round and round (or reincarnate), suffering again and again, as a blind person when led by the blind (priest).

1.2.09. Persons immersed in ignorance in various ways, flatter themselves by saying: We have accomplished life's purpose. These performers of rituals do not know the Truth due to their desires for enjoyment. They fall from heaven, misery-stricken, when the fruit of their work is exhausted.

1.2.10. Deluded ones, regarding sacrifices and unselfish humanitarian works as the highest, do not know any higher good. When they have exhausted their rewards in heaven gained by the good deeds, they enter again into this world or a lower one.

1.2.11. But those wise men of tranquil minds—who live in the forest (solitude) on alms, practicing austerity and deity worship become free from impurities—depart by the Northern Path to the abode of Brahmā.

Transcendental Knowledge leads to Liberation

1.2.12. Let the wise—after having examined all these worlds that are gained by rituals and humanitarian works—acquire freedom from desires and reflect that the **eternal Brahman cannot be obtained by non-eternal means** (such as rituals, Sevā). In order for him to understand the Eternal, let him approach a guru who is well versed in the Vedas and is a Self-realized soul (श्रोत्रिय ब्रह्मनिष्ठ).

Acquire this transcendental Knowledge from a Self-realized master by humble reverence, by sincere inquiry, and by service. The empowered ones, who have realized the Truth, will give you this Knowledge. **(BG 4.34)**

1.2.13. To the pupil who has respectfully approached him, whose mind is completely serene, and whose senses are under control; the Self-realized teacher will, indeed, impart the metaphysical science of Brahman, by which the immortal Purusha is known.

CHAPTER 2. Section 1

2.1.01. This is the Truth my good friend: As thousands of similar sparks come from a blazing fire, so also are various beings produced from the imperishable Brahman, and back to Him they go again.

2.1.02. He is the self-luminous and formless Absolute, uncreated and existing both inside and outside of creation. He is devoid of Prāna, devoid of human mind, pure, and higher than the eternal Brahman.

2.1.03. From Him are born Prāna(s), mind, all the sense-organs, Ākāsha (Ether), air, fire, water, and earth, which support all creatures.

2.1.04. The heavens are His head; the sun and moon, His eyes; the quarters (four directions), His ears; the revealed Vedas, His speech; the wind is His breath; the universe, His heart. From His feet is produced the earth. He is, indeed, the inner Self of all beings

2.1.05. From Him comes the Fire whose source is the sun; from the sun comes rain; from rain, the herbs that grow on the earth; from the herbs, the seminal fluid which a man pours into a woman. Thus many living beings are born of the Absolute.

2.1.06. From Him have come the Rik, the Sāma, the Yajur Vedas, the rites, all sacrifices, ceremonies, Knowledge, the time, the sacrificer, and the earth sustained by the sun and the moon.

Brahman is the source of every thing

2.1.07. From Him are born various devas, the celestials, men, cattle, birds, and also Prāna and apāna, rice and corn, penance, faith, truth, celibacy, and the laws.

2.1.08. From Him are born the seven Prānas, the seven flames, the seven kinds of fuel, the seven oblations, and also the seven worlds where Prānas move in the body of living beings.

2.1.09. From Him come all the oceans and the mountains; from Him flow all rivers; from Him come all plants and their saps, by which the subtle body (consisting of mind and intellect) subsists enshrined by the physical body. (Also see Gita Chapter 10)

Entering the earth, I support all beings with My energy. Becoming the sap-giving moon, I nourish all the plants and living beings. **(BG 15.**13)

2.1.10. Verily, the omnipresent Being alone is all this universe, work and austerity. O my good friend. He who knows this Brahman as the Supreme and immortal—hidden in the cavity of the causal heart—cuts down, even in this life, the knot of ignorance.

Section 2

Self is both with and without form

2.2.01. Brahman dwells and operates in the cavity of the causal heart. He supports all there is; everything that moves, breathes, and blinks is in Him. O disciples, know that Self is both with form (gross) and without form (subtle), He is adorable, Supreme, and beyond human understanding.

2.2.02. That which is radiant, subtler than the subtlest, That by which all the worlds and their inhabitants are supported—is the immortal Brahman; That is the Prāna, speech, and the mind; That is the Truth and the immortal. That alone is to be known. Know Him only, my friend.

The metaphor of bow, arrow and the target

2.2.03. Take the great weapon (**Om**) provided by the Upanishad as the bow, and place the arrow—the sharp and purified mind—on the bow. Then, draw back the arrow of mind from sense pleasures, fix the mind on the target (Brahman) and strike that imperishable target—Brahman; O my good friend.

What is the bow, arrow and the target is further summarized:

2.2.04. Contemplation on **Om** is the bow; mind is the arrow; Brahman is said to be the target. One should hit the target with an undistracted mind, and like the arrow let the mind become one with Brahman.

Knowledge of Brahman is the bridge to cross maya

2.2.05. The heaven, the earth, entire cosmos, the Prāna, the mind with all sense organs and sense objects, and everything else rests in Brahman. Know the non-dual Brahman only and give up all other talk. This Knowledge alone is the jiva's bridge to cross the ocean of maya (संसार-सागर) and reach the shore of immortality—Brahman.

2.2.06. Ātman operates within the heart where all the arteries meet like the spokes of a chariot wheel meet in the hub. Meditate solely on Ātman as Om. May He help you cross the ocean of ignorance (maya)!

2.2.07. He is all-knowing, all-wise, glorious and effulgent. He becomes the mind and leads the body and the senses. He dwells within every cell of the body and operates from inside the causal heart to keep the body alive and well. **By the Knowledge of the immortal Brahman the wise behold Him in all things and everywhere.**

2.2.08. When He is seen in both—the mortal and the immortal (क्षर और अक्षर), the saint and the sinner—all shackles (ego, desires, attachments etc.) are broken, all doubts are resolved, and all karma is burnt up. (Also see BG 4.37)

2.2.09. The wise know Him as the pure and indivisible Brahman, shining behind the bright, golden cover of maya. He is the Light of all lights.

2.2.10. The sun does not illumine Him, nor the moon and the stars, nor the lightning—how can this earthly fire illumine Him? Everything in the cosmos is illumined by His light.

(Also see KaU 5.15, ShU 6.14 and BG **15.06**)

2.2.11. Verily, this entire universe is the Supreme Brahman (ब्रह्मैवेदं विश्वमिदं वरिष्ठम्). He is everywhere—above and below, in the front and the back, on the right and the left. He alone pervades everything.

CHAPTER 3. Section 1
The analogy of two Birds

3.1.01. Two birds (Ishvara and jiva) of the same feather (related to each other), reside on the same tree (body). One of them (jiva) eats and enjoys the fruits of the tree, while the other (Ishvara) simply looks on as a witness, without eating the fruits. (Also see ShU 4.06)

The One and the same Spirit in the body is called the witness, the guide, the supporter, the enjoyer (Jiva), the great Lord and also the Supreme Self. (BG 13.22)

Two main aspects of Reality—the divine spark (Lord, Ishvara) and the living entity (individual soul, Jiva)—make their nest and reside on the same tree of the body as a part of the cosmic drama. Virtue and vice are the flowers of this tree; pains and pleasures of sense gratification are its sweet and sour fruits. The living entity, due to ignorance, becomes captivated by the fruits of the tree and gets attached to material Nature; eats these fruits and becomes subject to bondage and liberation; whereas the Lord sits on the tree, observes and guides the living entity. The Lord, being unattached to material Nature, remains free as a mere witness of the cosmic play. The Lord remains unaffected and unattached to the modes of material Nature just as a lotus leaf remains unaffected by water.

3.1.02. Seated on the same tree, one of them (jiva) sunk in ignorance and deluded, grieves. But when Jiva beholds the worshipful God and His glory, he becomes free from grief.

3.1.03. When the wise realizes the self-luminous Creator, the Lord, the Purusha, the progenitor of Brahmā; he becomes free from the evils of dualities—good and bad—and becomes pure. He finally becomes united with the supreme Reality.

3.1.04. He indeed is the Prāna that pervades all this. The wise man who knows Him does not engage in useless conversation. When one becomes free from confusion and delighted in the Self, he performs all actions for Him. Such a person is the foremost among the knowers of Brahman.

3.1.05. When the impurities fade away by unceasing practice of truthfulness, austerity, right Knowledge, and sense control—the wise behold the glorious and pure Ātman within his very body.

3.1.06. Only the good prevails over the evil in the end (सत्यमेव जयते नानृतम्). **By goodness is laid out the Divine Northern Path—the way to the gods—over which the seers, free from desires, ascend to the Supreme abode of Truth.**

Note 4: The word 'Truth' or 'Sat' also means God.

3.1.07. Vast, divine and beyond all imaginations, shines **Brahman—subtler than the subtlest and farther than the farthest. It is here within the body. The sages realize Him in this very life as dwelling in the bodies of all beings.**

3.1.08. Brahman cannot be described by words, nor perceived by the eyes and the senses, nor revealed by penance and rituals. When the mind becomes pure and serene by spiritual practices, then one realizes the Absolute by contemplation.

3.1.09. That subtle truth of Ātman is realized by means of the light of intellect within the body. The intellect is interwoven with the senses. **Thus, when the intellect is purified by Knowledge, Ātman shines forth. (Also see BG 3.43)**

3.1.10. Whatever world a man of pure Knowledge desires and whatever objects he cherishes, he obtains those worlds and those objects. Therefore let everyone, who wants spiritual progress, hold on to a hard to find Self-realized Guru.

Section 2

3.2.01. The Knower of the Self, knows that Supreme Abode of Brahman, which shines brightly and in which the universe rests.

Those wise men—without any material desire—who are devoted to such a Guru, go beyond rebirth.

3.2.02. Whoever longs for the objects of desire and broods over them, are reborn to fulfill those desires. But in the case of a sage, who becomes established in the Self, desires vanish away here in this very life and he has no further birth.

3.2.03. Atman is not attained through discourses or through intellect or through much learning. It is gained only by one who longs for it diligently (and qualifies for it). To such a person the Atman reveals its true nature. (Same as KaU 2.23)

3.2.04. This Ātman is not attained by one who is weak in faith and sincerity or by those who practice improper austerities. But wise men who strive with vigor, attention and sincerity attain union with Brahman.

3.2.05. Having realized Ātman, the seers become satisfied with the Supreme Knowledge. Their souls are established in the Supreme Self, they are free from passions, and their mind becomes tranquil. Such calm souls are ever devoted to the Self and behold everywhere the omnipresent Brahman and in the end enter into Him.

3.2.06. Becoming well established in the Self, the goal of the Vedāntic Knowledge, and having purified their minds through the practice of samnyāsa; the seers, never relaxing in their efforts, enjoy supreme peace on the earth and at the time of death attain Brahman.

3.2.07. The fifteen components (five basic elements and ten organs) that constitute jiva, go back to their sources after death, and the five sense objects to their deities; the actions and the Ātman reflected in the intellect, become one with the highest imperishable Brahman, which is the Self of all.

(Also see details of sixteen components or Kalās of Purusha mentioned in PrU 6.04)

3.2.08. As flowing rivers disappear in the sea, losing their names and forms, so a wise man, freed from name and form, attains the Purusha, who is the Greatest.

To know Brahman is to become Brahman

3.2.09. He who knows the Supreme Brahman verily becomes Brahman (ब्रह्मवेद ब्रह्मैव भवति). In his family no one is born ignorant of Brahman. When one becomes free from the impurities of his mind, he overcomes sorrow and sin, and becomes immortal. (Also see **BG 18.55**)

3.2.10. A Rik verse declares: This Knowledge of Brahman should be told only to those who have performed the necessary rituals, who are versed in the Vedas, devoted to Brahman, and who have faith and perform fire sacrifice.

To speak of wisdom to a deluded person, to glorify sacrifice to a greedy person, to advise sense control to an irascible person, and to discourse on Lord Rama's exploits to a lecher, is as useless as sowing seed on barren ground. One should not force others to believe. The study of the Bhagavad-Gita or any scripture is meant only for sincere persons. According to Shri Ramakrishna, one can understand Him as much as He makes one understand. Only they to whom He gives the divine Knowledge, in accordance with their karma, obtain it. (Also see **BG** 18.67).

3.2.11. Thus the seer Angiras declared this truth in ancient times. A man who has not taken the vow—or is not very serious—should not study this. Salutation to the great seers! Salutation to the great seers!

OM TAT SAT

Ādi Guru ShankarāChārya

6. MĀNDUKYA UPANISHAD

The **Māndukya Upanishad** is the shortest of the Upanishads. It belongs to the Atharvaveda group of Upanishads. It **is written in prose, consisting of just 12 verses** expounding the mystic mono syllable Om, the three psychological states of waking, dreaming and sleeping, and the transcendent Turiya state of illumination.

According to the Vedic theory of creation, the creation begins with the vibration of the primal energy that has a sound symbol, Om! **Om is ever considered the most suitable sound symbol of the Supreme Absolute**, with the help of which a devotee can realize the Truth. It is the first sound, representing both visible and invisible, in the creation.

Om is transliterated as AUM. A is the first sound made by a baby coming out of mother's womb. It is also the first letter in most of the languages. It is the most important vowel in Indo-European languages. No consonant can be pronounced without adding the vowel "a, अ" in the end of it. Thus A is chosen as the first letter in AUM and is related to the visible creation, the external objects. This is the first state of consciousness. This is also called the wakeful state of the self, Jiva or mind. Letter U represents dream state and letter M stands for deep sleep state of the self.

Om is the sacred syllable representing Brahman, the impersonal Absolute of Hinduism—omnipotent, omnipresent, and the source of all manifest existence. Brahman, in itself, is incomprehensible; so a symbol becomes mandatory to help us realize the Unknowable. Om, therefore, represents both the unmanifest (nirguna) and manifest (saguna) aspects of God. That is why it is called pranava, to mean that it pervades life and runs through our Prāna (breath).

What does 'Om' mean?

Om is the sacred sound that is considered to be the greatest of all Vedic mantras.

This mono syllable Om is composed of the **three sounds** A-U-M (in Sanskrit, the vowels a and u combine to become o). The symbol's threefold nature is central to its meaning. Everything is contained in It:

- "A" for **Action** of creation (Brahmā).
- "U" for **Upholding, and preservation (**Vishnu).
- "M" for destructive power of **Mahesha.**
- Three worlds—Earth, Planets, and Galaxies (भूः, भुवः, स्वः).

- Three sacred Vedas—Rig, Yajur, and Sāma.

- Three names of God (Om Tat Sat).
- Three Gunas of Nature.
- Three aspects of Reality: Sat, Chit, Ānanda.
- O' ham, sa Om (ओंऽहम् स ॐ). That which I am, is Om.
- When God decides to create, "Om" is heard. Thus everything has its origin in "Om."

Thus Om, mystically embodies the **essence of the entire universe**. This meaning is deepened further by the Indian philosophical belief that God first created sound and the universe arose from it. As the most sacred sound, Om is the root of the universe and everything that exists. This sacred sound continues to hold everything together.

When one leaves the physical body, by controlling all the senses, focusing the mind on God and the bioimpulses (Life forces, Prāna) in the cerebrum, engaged in yogic practice, meditating on Me, and uttering Om—the sacred monosyllable cosmic sound power of the Spirit—one attains the Supreme Abode. (**BG** 8.12-13)

The sound of 'Om' or 'AUM' is a combination of three primary sounds: A, U, and M. It is the source of all sounds one can utter. Therefore, it is the fittest sound symbol of Spirit. It is also the primeval impulse that moves our five nerve centers that control bodily functions. The Vedas says: Om is the original sound, the first word spoken by God, and by which all that "IS" was created, and is being sustained and evolved at this very moment. The Bible paraphrased the same: In the beginning was the word (Amen) and the word was with God, and the word was God (John 1.01). "Om is not counted among words," said Sri Ramakrishna. "It is not a word, it is God Himself," said Swami Vivekananda. There are several names of the Absolute; **Om** is the shortest generic (or universal) name of the Source of the universe.

Āgama Prakarana (The Preface)

01. Harih Om! The whole universe is Om! A further explanation is this: All that is in the past, present and future is, indeed, Om! And whatever else there is—beyond the threefold division of time—that also is just Om!

Om is Brahman vibrating eternally in the Ether. It reveals all that is to be known: Brahman Itself. Om is life, Om is Cosmos, Om is both Saguna and Nirguna aspects of Brahman. The meditation techniques given on pages 58 to 60—if practiced with sincerity and deep love for Om—will gradually open the petals of Cosmic flower that we all are.

02. All this is, indeed, Brahman. This Ātman (or Jivātman, the Self, within the body) is the same as Brahman (अयमात्मा ब्रह्म). The Self or Consciousness has four parts or states.

Note 5: The word Ātman or Ātmā in Vedānta stands for Jivātmā which is an integral part of Brahman. The Self and the self are the same.

03. The self in the waking state is also called Vaishvānara, who is conscious of external objects, who has seven limbs and nineteen mouths and experiences gross (material) sense objects. This is the first state of consciousness.

04. The self seated in the dream state is called Taijasa, who is conscious of internal (mental) objects, who is also endowed with seven limbs and nineteen mouths and who enjoys the subtle objects of mental-world. This is the second state of consciousness.

Note 6: The seven limbs of the macroCosmic being (समष्टि) are: The space as the main body, the head as heavens, the suns as eyes, fire as mouth, the air as Prāna, water as the belly and the planets are the legs.

Note 7: The nineteen mouths of the microCosmic being (व्यष्टि) are: five sense organs (nose, tongue, eye, skin and ear); five organs of action (mouth, hand, leg, anus, and urethra); five Prānas, and the four subtle organs (अन्तःकरण)—mind, intellect, chitta and ego.

05. The Self present in the deep sleep state is called Prajnā (intellect, प्रज्ञा) at personal (व्यष्टि) level and Ishvara at universal (समष्टि) level where a sleeper neither desires any object nor sees any dream. All experiences become unified and full of consciousness and (temporary) bliss. This is the gateway to the remembrance of all three states. This is the third state of consciousness.

06. Ishvara is the Lord of all three states. He is the knower of all. He is the inner controller. He is the source of all; from Him all beings originate and in Him they finally disappear.

Note 8: This is a description of our own personal level of prajñā during deep sleep as well as the **universal Prajñā, Ishvara** or Brahman. In deep sleep all experiences, education, sorrow etc. is dissolved and after waking up everything is created as it was.

Three States of individual Consciousness

THREE STATES	1. Individual (व्यष्टि) or Microcosmic level	2. Universal (समष्टि) or Macrocosmic level
(1) Waking state **(Physical body)** **Beta** Brain waves >8Hz or cycles/sec	Vaishvānara(Vishva) **Physical/ body level**. letter A (अ)of AUM	Virāt or Cosmic body/ cosmos. (BG, Ch. 11)
(2) Dream state **(Subtle body)** **Theta** Brain waves 4-8 Hz (REM state)	Taijasa (Brilliant) **Mental/ mind level.** Letter U (उ)of AUM	HiranyaGarbha, The **Cosmic mind** in seed or egg form.
(3) Deep Sleep **(Causal body**, seed, Samskāra) **Delta** brain waves 1-4 Hz	Prajñā, Conscious-ness or **Intellect level**, letter M (म्) of AUM	Creator (Ishvara), Controller, God, **Brahman.**
The Turiya state Non-dual existence Brain waves 0.2-1 Hz	Self-realized or **Soul level.** Jnāna-Samādhi, ओम्	ParaBrahman, The Absolute, **Source** ॐ Om

The three states are also related to our three bodies:

(1) Physical body consists of body and all supporting organs.

(2) Astral or subtle body consists of mind, intellect and ego.

(3) Causal body: This is the storehouse of karmic records, known as Samskāra. In waking state all three bodies are active, working together and are attached by the chord of Prāna.

In dream state, physical body gets separated from the other two bodies (subtle and causal). In this state, physical body and its organs are at rest, but mind (subtle body #2) and causal body #3 remains active. Mind creates a replacement dream body to do dream actions called dreaming. In this state only bodies (2) and (3) are active, working together and are connected by Prāna.

In the deep sleep state, mind also becomes inactive and all three bodies get separated and become non-active. This is a state of temporary freedom (Mukti) for jiva. One enjoys complete rest, gets refreshed and enjoys peace. The chord of Prāna keeps the physical body alive in idling mode. If this chord breaks, the body becomes dead. **Three bodies are kept alive by the chord of Prāna in all three states of consciousness.** In deep sleep state the three bodies are not connected with each other, they are only connected by the chord of Prāna. And in death the chord of Prāna is also cut; subtle and causal bodies together with Prāna leave the physical body that becomes dead and contains four basic elements. These basic elements also go to their source, the Ākāsha (ether or God), when cremation takes place and one life cycle of Jiva ends. **Om!**

Turiya or Super-Conscious State

07. The Fourth (or Turiya) state is thought of as that which is not conscious of the internal world, nor conscious of the external world, nor conscious of both the worlds, nor dense with consciousness, nor simple consciousness, nor unconsciousness. It is unperceived, unrelated, **incomprehensible, unthinkable and indescribable. It is the essence of Consciousness manifesting as the self in all three states,** It is the end of all experience; it is all peace, all bliss and non-dual. This Brāhmic state has to be realized and is called Turiya/ Super-conscious state.

The truth about the transcendental state of Turiya cannot really be described by or taught to anyone—it has to arise by itself as a result of the individual drawing nearer to the Self. It is a matter of spiritual evolution.

The individual self has been sleeping in the darkness of ignorance created by maya from time immemorial. **When jiva wakes up at the dawn of Knowledge (in Turiya) after many many lives, the world and its objects look unreal like dream objects to him even while he is physically awake!** The Turiya state is permanent Jnāna-Samādhi as opposed to temporary Dhyāna-Samādhi. In this state one realizes that waking world is also a **transcendental dream world.** He comes to realize that the world is not as one sees, and what it really is cannot be seen, except in Turiya state. The world of duality exists only due to deep-rooted ignorance created by maya (माया मात्रं इदं द्वैतम्).

The Creator, Creation and Jiva (Jiva, Jagat and Jagadisha) are one and the same with different forms and names. To perceive the existence of Ātman only in the universe is Moksha.

Note 9: The Turiya state is not a state in a real sense, it is the Supreme Goal of life, the end of all states where world disappears even in waking state, and one sees Brahman only!

08. That same Self, from the point of view of the single syllable is Om! The Om with parts is viewed from the stand-point of three letters (A, U and M). The states are the letters, and the letters are the states. And the letters are A, U and M.

09. Vaishvānara Ātman, whose sphere of activity is the waking state, is A, the first letter of AUM, on account of his all-pervasiveness or being the **first** alphabet. He who knows this obtains all desires and becomes the **first** among the great.

No sound can be produced without opening the mouth and the **first sound** produced on opening the mouth is 'A'. Hence 'A' is all pervasive and the first letter of most languages and the first sound of a newborn child. The waking state precedes dream and sleep states.

10. Taijasa Ātman, whose sphere of activity is the dream state, is U, the second letter of AUM, and it comes in between A and M. Letter 'U' is said to be **superior** only apparently, because it comes just after 'A'. He who knows all this[9] attains a **superior Knowledge of Brahman**, receives equal treatment from all and finds no one in his family ignorant of Brahman.

[9] **The dream or REM state comes between waking and deep sleep.** REM means Rapid Eye Movement. It is a state of half sleep when you are dreaming and your eyes move rapidly.

11. Consciousness present in the state of deep sleep is M, the last letter of the word 'AUM'. Because of M being the entity wherein A and U seem to **merge** or become **absorbed** into M. He who knows all this[10] is **able to absorb and comprehend** all Knowledge within himself.

[10] Waking and dream seem to merge into deep sleep.

12. That **Om**—which is without letters (**mono-syllable**) representing all three states—is the Turiya state, beyond comprehension by ordinary means, the cessation of the extraordinary world, the auspicious and the non-dual. Thus Om is verily the Self. This Om is verily Ātman. He who knows all this merges his self in the Self.

OM TAT SAT

A BASIC MEDITATION-1 (For the Beginners)

A simple technique of meditation is described here: **(1)** Sit in a clean, quiet, dark place; in any comfortable posture with head, neck, and spine straight and vertical. Make sure before starting the process that breathing is equalized using alternate breathing or any other technique.

(1) No music or incense during meditation is recommended. The time and place of meditation should be fixed. Midnight, morning, and evening are the best times to meditate for 15 to 20 minutes every day. **(2)** Remember any name or form of the personal god (Ishta Deva) you believe in, and ask His or Her blessings. **(3)** Close your eyes, take 5 to 10 very slow and deep breaths. **(4)** Fix your gaze, mind, and feelings inside the chest center, the seat of the causal heart, and breathe slowly. Mentally chant "So" as you breathe in and "ham" as you breathe out. Think as if breath itself is making these sounds "So" and "ham". Mentally visualize the breath going in and coming out through the nostrils. Do not try to control or lead your breathing; just watch your natural breathing. **(5)** Direct the will towards the thought of merging yourself into the infinite space of the air you are breathing that is full of sound waves with the symbol of **Om like this :** ...ॐॐॐ...

If mind starts to wander, start from step **(3)** again.

TAITTIRIYA UPANISHAD

The **Taittiriya Upanishad** is associated with the Taittiriya School of the Yajurveda. It figures as number 7 in the Muktika list of 108 Upanishads. It has three chapters and several sections dealing with diverse subjects. It has about **52 paragraphs** written in prose.

CHAPTER 1. LESSON ON LEARNING

Section 1. Invocation

Harih Om! May Mitra be auspicious to us! May Varuna be auspicious to us! May Aryaman be auspicious to us! May Indra and Brihaspati be auspicious to us! May Vishnu, of wide steps, be auspicious to us! Salutation to Brahman! Salutation to You, O Vāyu! You indeed are the visible Brahman. I shall proclaim You as the visible Brahman. O Vāyu, I shall proclaim You as the right. I shall proclaim You as the true.

May it protect me! May it protect the teacher! May it protect me! May it protect the teacher! Om! Shantih! Shantih! Shantih!

Section 2. Lesson on pronunciation

Om! We shall now explain the science of enunciation. It consists of the alphabets, accent, quality, articulation, modulation, and continuity in pronouncing the letters. Thus is explained the six limbs of the lesson on pronunciation.

Section 3. Reflection on the combinations

1.3.01. May glory come to both of us together! May the light of Brahman shine alike through both of us! Now we shall explain the teaching of the **combinations** under **five headings**: The **worlds**, the **heavenly lights**, **Knowledge**, **progeny** and the **body**.

1.3.02. First, with regard to the **worlds**: The earth is the first form, heaven is the second from, the ākāsha is the union and the air is the medium. Thus one should contemplate upon the universe.

1.3.03. Next, with regard to the **heavenly lights**: Fire is the first form, the sun is the second form, water is the union and lightning is the medium. Thus one should contemplate upon the heavenly lights.

1.3.04. Next, with regard to **Knowledge**: The teacher is the first form, the pupil is the second form, Knowledge is the union and instruction is the means of joining them, the medium. Thus is with regard to Knowledge.

1.3.05. Next, with regard to **progeny**: The mother is the first form, the father is the second form, the progeny is the union and procreation is the medium.

1.3.06. Next, with regard to the **body**: The lower lip is the first form, the upper lip is the second form, the speech is the union and the tongue is the medium.

The five great combinations

Headings	First form	Second form	Intermediate form, union	Means of joining
Worlds	earth	heaven	space	air
Luminaries	fire	sun	water	lightning
Knowledge	teacher	student	Knowledge	instruction
Progeny	mom	dad	progeny	reproduction
Body	Lower lip	Upper lip	speech	tongue

1.3.07. These are the great Samhitās (collection of Vedic mantras). He who meditates on these Samhitās, as explained above, becomes united with progeny, cattle, the light of Brahman, food and the heavenly world.

Section 4. The Universal prayer

1.4.01. May He who is the bull of the Vedic hymns, who assumes all forms, who has sprung from the immortal hymns of the Vedas—may God give me wisdom. O God, may I be the possessor of immortality! May my body be competent; may my tongue be exceedingly sweet; may I hear abundantly with my ears. You are the sheath of Brahman, concealed by intelligence. Guard for me what I have learned.

1.4.02. Om! Next bring to me, without delay, fortune accompanied by wool and cattle—fortune which always provides me with clothes and cattle, food and drink. Increase them when they have been acquired and preserve them for long when increased. Svāhā! May celibates come to me! Svāhā! May celibates come to me! Svāhā! May celibates practice self-control! Svāhā! May celibates enjoy peace! Svāhā!

1.4.03. May I become famous among men! Svāhā! May I become richer than the rich! Svāhā! O gracious Lord, may I enter into You! Svāhā! May You, O gracious Lord, enter into me! Svāhā! O Lord, I am cleansing my sins in that Self of Your's, which is like a river of a thousand branches. Svāhā! O Preserver, as water flow downward, as the months merge into a year, so may students of Brahma-vidyā come to me from everywhere. Svāhā!

Note 10: In the above payer the rishi is praying not only for himself, but for the welfare of all creatures.

The Universal Vedic Prayer

ॐ सर्वे भवन्तु सुखिनः, सर्वे सन्तु निरामयाः । सर्वे भद्राणि पश्यन्तु, मा कश्चित् दुःख भाग्भवेत् ॥

Om! Sarve bhavantu sukhinah	May all be prosperous and happy
Sarve santu nirāmayāh	May all be free from illness
Sarve bhadrāni pashyantu	May all see what is spiritually uplifting
Mā kashchit duhkha bhāgbhavet	May no one suffer

Om! Shāntih! Shāntih! Shāntih!

Section 5. Description of Four Great Utterances

1.5.01. Bhuh, Bhuvah, Svah—these are the three great utterances (महाव्याहृतियां) chanted during Vedic rituals and upāsanās. Besides these there is **a fourth one**, called **Mahah**, which became known to the son of Mahāchamasa. That **Mahah** is Brahman, that is the Self. The other gods are its limbs.

1.5.02. Bhuh is, verily, this **earth**; Bhuvah, the **planets**; Svah, the **galaxies**; Mahah, **the sun**. Through the sun, indeed, all the worlds are nourished. (in stage 1)

1.5.03. Bhuh is, verily, **fire**; Bhuvah, the **air**; Svah, the **sun**; Mahah, the **moon**. By the moon light, indeed, do all creatures get their nourishing crop to thrive. (in stage 2)

1.5.04. Bhuh is, verily, the **Rik verses**; Bhuvah, **the Sāman**; Svah, **the Yajus**; Mahah, **Brahman**. By Brahman, indeed, do all the Vedas came. (in stage 3)

1.5.05. Bhuh is, verily, the **Prāna**, Bhuvah, the **apāna**; Svah, the **vyāna**; Mahah, **food**. By food, indeed, do all living beings (**prāni**) thrive. (in stage 4)

1.5.06. These above mentioned four are themselves fourfold: the four vyāhritis are each described in four different stages as given below in a tabular form below. He who knows these knows Brahman. All the gods bring offerings to him.

Description of utterances (vyāhritis)

Vyāhritis	Stage 1	Stage 2	Stage 3	Stage 4
Bhuh	Earth	Fire	Rik	Prāna
Bhuvah	Planets	Air	Sāma	Apāna
Svah	Galaxies	Sun	Yajur	Vyāna
Mahah	Cosmos	Moon	Om	Food

Section 6. Reflection on saguna Brahman

1.6.01. There is a space within the causal heart; in it resides the intelligent, immortal, luminous Purusha. The Sushumnā passes through the piece of flesh—a cherry-size **pituitary gland**—which hangs down like a nipple between the two palates and ends where the skull splits and the roots of hair lie apart. That Sushumnā is the path for the realization of God. The souls of the aspirants, passing through the Sushumnā, rest in the fire, represented by the vyāhriti Bhuh; and also rest in the air, represented by the vyāhriti Bhuvah.

1.6.02. He rests in the sun, represented by the vyāhriti Svah; he rests in Brahman, represented by the vyāhriti Mahah. He attains the Self. He attains the lordship of the mind; he attains the lordship of speech; he attains the lordship of sight; he attains the lordship of hearing; he attains the lordship of intelligence. Furthermore, he becomes Brahman, whose body is space, whose nature is existence (SAT), who sports in life as Prāna, whose mind is bliss, who is full of peace, who is immortal. Thus one should meditate on saguna or visible Brahma.

Section 7. Reflection on fivefold nature

1.7.01. The earth, planets, galaxies (heaven), the four directions (North, South. East and West) and the intermediate directions. Agni (fire), Vāyu (air), Aditya (sun), Chandramā (moon) and the Nakshatras (stars). Water, herbs, tree, space and the body—So much with reference to material objects. Now with reference to the body: The Prāna, apāna, vyāna, udāna and samāna; the eye, the ear, the mind, speech and touch; the skin, flesh, muscle, bone and marrow. Having thus instructed, Rishi said: "Whatever exists is fivefold." The one set of fivefold grouping sustains the other set of fivefold in the group.

Divinity pervades and sustains the entire universe of multiplicity as mentioned in the Gita: Everything in the universe is strung on Me like different thread-beads are strung on a garland made of thread (**BG** 7.07).

Section 8. Reflection on OM

Om is Brahman. Om is all this. This syllable Om is uttered to indicate approval. When they are told: "recite Om," they recite. Uttering Om, they sing the Sāman chants. With "Om Som" they recite the prayers. Uttering Om, the atharvan priest gives the response. Uttering Om, the Brahman gives approval. Uttering Om, gives permission to offer oblations in the Agnihotra (purifying fire sacrifice from the ancient science of Āyurveda). When a Vedic teacher wishes to obtain Brahman he utters Om; thus desiring Brahman, he verily obtains Brahman.

Section 9. Disciplines

Learning and propagating the truths of the Vedas are to be practiced along with: righteousness, austerity, sense-control, tranquility, the kindling of sacrificial fires, the performance of the Agnihotra sacrifice, hospitality to guests, the performance of social duties and **procreation and propagation of the race**. All these are to be practiced sincerely.

There are differing views on the subject: **righteousness alone**, according to Satyvachas of the line of Rathitara, should be practiced; **austerity alone**, according to Taponitya the son of Purusishti; according to Naka, the learning and teaching of the **Vedas alone**, for that is austerity.

Section 10. A mantra for daily contemplation

1.10.01. Trisanku proclaimed after the attainment of the Knowledge of the Self: I am the mover of the tree of the universe. My fame rises high, like a mountain peak. My root is the Supremely Pure Brahman. I am the unstained essence of the Self, like the nectar of immortality that resides in the sun. I am the brightest treasure. I am the shinning wisdom. I am immortal and imperishable. *(Lord Krishna also used 'I' in the sense of the Self in many verses of the Gita.)*

Section 11. Advice to the students

1.11.01. Speak the truth. Practice dharma. Do not neglect the study of the Vedas. Having brought to the teacher the gift (Guru Dakshina or guru's fee) desired by him, **enter the householder's life and see that the line of progeny is not cut off. Do not swerve from the truth. Do not swerve from dharma. Do not neglect personal welfare. Do not neglect prosperity. Do not neglect the study, practice and the propagation of teachings of the Vedas.**

1.11.02. Do not neglect your duties to the gods and the Manes (souls of deceased ancestors). **Treat your mother as god. Treat your father as god. Treat your teacher as god. Treat your guest as god.** Whatever deeds are faultless, these are to be performed, not others. Whatever good works have been performed by us, those should be performed by you, not others.

1.11.03. Those brāhmanas who are superior to us—you should comfort them by giving them seats. **Whatever is to be given should be given with faith, not without faith—according to one's capacity to give, with modesty, without fear, and with sympathy.**

Read more on three types of charity as given in the Gita verses (17.20-21) on www.gita-society.com/explanationRead.html

1.11.04. Now, if there arises in your mind any doubt concerning any act, or any doubt concerning conduct, you should conduct yourself in such a manner as brāhmanas would conduct themselves—brāhmanas who are competent to judge, who of their own accord are devoted to good deeds and are not urged to their performance by others, and who are not too difficult, but are lovers of dharma. Now, with regards to persons who speak against, you should conduct yourself in such a way as brāhmanas would conduct themselves—brāhmanas who are competent to judge, who of their own accord are devoted to good deeds and are not urged to their performance by others, and who are not cruel, but are lovers of dharma. This is the rule. This is the teaching. This is the secret wisdom of the Vedas. This is the command of God. This alone should be observed.

Section 12. The peace chant

May all the Devas be auspicious to us and protect me and protect the students.   **Om! Shantih! Shantih! Shantih!**

CHAPTER 2. BRAHMĀNANDA, THE BLISS OF BRAHMAN
(The Five Sheaths (koshas, coverings) of Ātman)

Section 1. The sheath of food or body

Om! May Brahman protect us both! May Brahman bestow upon us both the fruit of Knowledge! May we both obtain the energy to acquire Knowledge! May what we both study reveal the Truth! May we cherish no ill-feeling toward each other! **Om! Shantih! Shantih! Shantih!**

2.1.01. Om! He who knows Brahman attains the Supreme. On the above, the following mantra is recorded: **"He who knows Brahman is Reality, Knowledge and Infinite (सत्यं ज्ञानं अनन्तम् ब्रह्म), hidden in the cavity of the causal heart and in the highest ākāsha—he, being one with the omniscient Brahman, gets all desires immediately fulfilled (or becomes desireless) and enjoys the Supreme Bliss (Ānandam)."**

2.1.02. From the Ātman was born Ākāsha (or Ādi Prakriti); from Ākāsha, air; from air, fire; from fire, water; from water, earth; from earth, herbs; from herbs, food; from food, man.

2.1.03. This physical body is made up of the essence of food. Food, indeed, is the head, right arm, left arm, the body and the legs or the tail. *(The whole physical body is made up of food.)*

Section 2. The sheath of the Prāna

2.2.01. "From food, verily, are produced all creatures—whatsoever dwell on earth. By food alone, furthermore, do they live and to food, in the end, do they return; for food alone is the eldest of all created beings and therefore, it is called the "cure all, panacea (Annam)." *(Proper food is called the best medicine)*

They who worship food as Brahman obtain all food. Food alone is the eldest of all beings and therefore it is called the panacea for all. From food all creatures are born: by food, when born, they grow. Because it is eaten by beings and because improper food eats beings, therefore it is called food.

The etymology of the word 'annam' is: "That which is eaten and that which eats". The higher form of life uses the lower form of life as food for sustenance. **One living being is food for another** (जीवो जीवस्य जीवनम्) **(MB 12.15.20, BP 1.13.47).** The eater and the eaten are one and the same.

2.2.02. Verily, different from this, which consists of the essence of food, but within it, is another self, which consists of the vital breath (Prāna). **The sheath of food (the physical body) is supported by Prāna.** This too has the shape of a man. Like the human shape of the former, is the human shape of the latter. Prāna, indeed, is its head; vyāna is its right wing; apāna is its left wing; ākāsha is its trunk; the earth is its tail, its support. (Prānas fully occupy the body, thus its shape is same as body it enters.)

Section 3. The sheath of the mind

2.3.01. "The gods also live by Prāna, so also do men and cattle; for the Prāna is the life of all beings. Therefore it is called the **universal life of all.** Those who worship the Prāna as Brahman obtain a full life.

2.3.02. This sheath of the **Prāna supports the body.** And is different from this sheath of body; within the sheath of Prāna, is another self, which consists of the mind. **The Prāna is supported by the mind.** This mind sheath too has the shape of a man. Like the human shape of the former is the human shape of the latter. The Yajurveda is its head, the Rigveda is its right wing, the Sāmaveda is its left wing, the teaching is its trunk, the hymns of Atharvaveda and Angiras are its tail, its support.

Section 4. The sheath of the intellect

2.4.01. He who knows the Bliss of Brahman, which is beyond the reach of the mind and speech, is not afraid of anything whatsoever. The mind supports Prāna and is being supported by the intellect. (A similar verse is in TaU 2.9.1)

2.4.02. The sheath of the **mind supports and guides the Prāna.** Verily, different from this sheath of mind, but within it, is another self, which consists of the intellect. **The mind is supported by the intellect.** This also has the shape of a man. Like the human shape of the former is the human shape of the latter. Faith is its head, what is right is its right wing, what is truth is its left wing, yoga is the trunk, Mahah (the **Cosmic Intellect**) is its tail, and its support.

Section 5. The sheath of Knowledge and Bliss

2.5.01. The Knowledge performs all the sacrifices; it also accomplishes all actions. All the gods worship the Knowledge, who is the eldest, as Brahman. If one knows the Knowledge as Brahman and if he does not depart from it, he is freed from all evils and desires, and becomes Blissful!

2.5.02. Verily, different from Knowledge, but within the Knowledge, is another self, which consists of **Bliss.** Bliss supports Knowledge and **Bliss is supported by the Ātmā or Brahman.** This also has the shape of a man[**]. Like the human shape of the former is the human shape of the latter. Joy is its head, delight is its right arm, great delight is its left arm, Bliss is its trunk. Brahman is its leg and its support.

*(** Note: Knowledge and Bliss, intellect, mind, and Prāna pervade every cell of the body-container and are not localized. They take the shape of the container they enter.)*

Section 6. Brahman: Source, support and sink of all

2.6.01. "If a person knows Brahman as non-existent, he himself becomes non-existent (or the atheist misses the goal of human birth and perishes). If he knows Brahman as existent, then he knows himself as existent." Brahman exists and supports all.

The irrational, the faithless, and the disbeliever (atheist) perish (or transmigrate). There is neither this world nor the world beyond nor happiness for a disbeliever. **(BG** 4.40)

In the hierarchy of support, the higher supports and guides the lower ones:

Brahman > Knowledge/Bliss > intellect > mind > Prāna > body

Thus, Brahman is the ultimate **source and support** of all its five coverings as discussed and shown above.

2.6.02. Thereupon the following questions arise: Does the ignorant, after leaving this world, go There? or, does the Knower, after leaving this world, obtain That Supreme Being?

Note 11: The answer to this question is left to be discovered by the students. This question implies a doubt as to what is the special benefit derived by spiritual endeavor, when every born creature would ultimately merge back to the Source, the world is a mere divine drama, and we are just a divine instrument!

2.6.03. He desired: "May I be many, may I be born. He performed austerities. Having performed austerities (tapas, deep thinking, brooding), He created all this, whatever there is. Having created all this, He entered into it. Having entered into it, He became both the manifest and the unmanifest, both the defined and undefined, both the supported and unsupported, both the intelligent and the non-intelligent, both the real and the unreal. The SAT or Brahman became all this.

Section 7. Brahman as fearlessness

2.7.01. "In the beginning all this was non-existent or invisible Brahman. From It was born what exists. Brahman created itself by itself; therefore it is called the self-made (स्वंभू)."

2.7.02. That which is Self-made is an object of joy; for truly, on knowing the joy (Bliss, Brahman) one becomes blissful and fearless. **Who could direct the Prāna and the Apāna if this Bliss did not exist in the cavity of the heart? Brahman verily exists, because it alone bestows bliss.**

2.7.03. When a man finds fearless support in That which is invisible, spiritual, indefinable and supportless, he has then obtained fearlessness (of transmigration and becomes immortal, and Blissful!).

If one makes even the slightest differentiation between Brahman and His creation, there is fear of death for him. That becomes fear for the knower also who does not understand (or reflect on) Brahman very well. (Here is a partial answer to the question posed earlier in verse **2.6.2**.)

Section 8. Brahmānanda, the Bliss of Brahman

2.8.01. "From fear of Him the wind blows; from fear of Him the sun rises; from fear of Him Agni, Indra and Death, the fifth, do their respective duties." (Also see KaU 6.02)

2.8.02. The following is the inquiry regarding the Bliss (of Knowing Brahman, Brahmānanda-Rasa). Suppose there is a young man—a noble young man, the best of rulers, firm in body and strong and possesses the whole world, full of wealth. That is one unit of human bliss. This **human bliss**, multiplied one hundred times, is one unit of the bliss of the **human gandharvas**. This also is less than or equal to the bliss of a follower of the Vedas who is free from all desires.

2.8.03. This bliss of the human gandharvas, multiplied one hundred times, is one unit of the bliss of the **celestial gandharvas**. This also is less than or equal to the bliss of a follower of the Vedas who is free from all desires.

2.8.04. This bliss of the celestial gandharvas, multiplied one hundred times, is one unit of the bliss of the **Manes**, who dwell in the long-enduring world. This also is less than or equal to the bliss of a follower of the Vedas who is free from all desires.

2.8.05. This bliss of the Manes who dwell in the long-enduring world, multiplied one hundred times, is one unit of the bliss of the **gods born in the Ajana heaven.** This also is less than or equal to the bliss of a follower of the Vedas who is free from all desires.

2.8.06. The bliss of the gods born in the Ajana heaven, multiplied one hundred times, is one unit of the bliss of the **sacrificial gods** who have attained divinity by means of sacrifices. This also is less than or equal to the bliss of a follower of the Vedas who is free from all desires.

2.8.07. The bliss of the sacrificial gods, multiplied one hundred times, is one unit of the **bliss of the gods**. This also is less than or equal to the bliss of a follower of the Vedas who is free from all desires.

2.8.08. The bliss of the gods, multiplied one hundred times, is one unit of the **bliss of Indra**. This also is less than or equal to the bliss of a follower of the Vedas who is free from all desires.

2.8.09. The bliss of Indra, multiplied one hundred times, is one unit of the **bliss of Brihaspati**. This also is less than or equal to the bliss of a follower of the Vedas who is free from all desires.

2.8.10. The bliss of Brihaspati, multiplied one hundred times, is one unit of the bliss of Prajāpati, **Brahmā**. This also is less than or equal to the bliss of a follower of the Vedas who is free from all desires.

2.8.11. The bliss of Brahmā, multiplied one hundred times, is one unit of the **bliss of Brahman** (ब्रह्मानन्द). This equals the bliss of a follower of the Vedas who becomes **absolutely free** from all desires.

Note: The gist of verses 02 to 11 is: There is no bliss equal to or greater than the bliss of a very sincere follower of the teachings of the Vedas (or a Self-realized soul) who becomes free from all desires. The degree of Bliss depends on the degree of desirelessness attained.

2.8.12. He who is here in man and he who is in the sun—both are one and the same. He who fully understands this before leaving this world, attains the Self which consists of food, attains the self which consist of the vital breath, attains the self which consists of the mind, attains the self which consists of intellect, attains the self which consists of bliss.

Section 9. The merging of good and evil

2.9.01. He who knows the Bliss of Brahman, which is beyond the reach of mind and speech, is no more afraid of anything whatsoever. (A similar verse is in TaU 2.4.1)

2.9.02. He does not distress himself with the thought: **Why did I not do what is good? Why did I do what is evil? Whosoever knows the Truth, regards all work as the work of Nature and not his own work.** (Also see BG 3.27). Such, indeed, is the power of the teachings of Upanishads, the secret Knowledge of Brahman.

CHAPTER 3. VARUNA-BHRIGU DIALOGUE

Section 1. Definition of Brahman

Om! May Brahman protect us both! May Brahman bestow upon us both the fruit of Knowledge! May we both obtain the energy to acquire Knowledge! May what we both study reveal the Truth! May we cherish no ill-feeling toward each other.

Om! Shantih! Shantih! Shantih!

3.1.01. Harih Om! Bhrigu, the son of Varuna, approached his father Varuna and said: "Venerable Sir, teach me about Brahman." Varuna said this to Bhrigu: **"Food, the vital breath, the eyes, the ears, the mind and the speech—are Brahman". To him he said further: "That from which these beings are born, That by which, when born, they live, That into which they enter, they merge. That is Brahman. Seek to know That by austerities."**

Bhrigu performed austerities (tapas). Having performed austerities— (Also see MuU 1.1.08 for a definition of tapas)

Section 2. The body as Brahman

He realized that **food is Brahman**; for from food, verily, are these beings born; by food, when born, do they live; into food they merge. Having realized this, he approached his father again and said: "Venerable Sir, teach me Brahman."

To him, the son, he said this: "Seek to know Brahman by means of austerities (तपसा ब्रह्म विजिज्ञासस्व) or Tapas, deep concentration or thinking on Brahman. For austerities (Tapas) are the only means of knowing Brahman." He practiced austerities.

Tapas does not mean torturing of the body as popularized in the Purānas. It is deep thinking of Brahman to know Him.

Section 3. The Prāna as Brahman

Having practiced austerities— He realized that the **Prāna is Brahman**; for from the Prāna, verily, are these beings born; by the Prāna, when born, do they live; into the Prāna do they enter, do they merge. Having realized this, he approached his father again and said: "Venerable Sir, teach me Brahman."

To him, the son, he said this: "Seek to know Brahman by means of austerities. For austerities are the means of knowing Brahman." He practiced austerities. Having practiced austerities—

Section 4. The mind as Brahman

He realized that the **mind is Brahman**; for from the mind, verily, are these beings born; by the mind, when born, do they live; into the mind, at the time of dissolution, do they enter, do they merge. *(The mind is also called maya or Prakriti.)*

Having realized this, he approached his father again and said: "Venerable Sir, teach me Brahman."

To him, the son, he said this: "Seek to know Brahman by means of austerities; for austerities are Brahman." He practiced austerities. Having practiced austerities—

Section 5. The intellect as Brahman

He realized that the **intellect is Brahman**; because, from the intellect of Brahman (Brahmā), verily, are these beings born; by the intellect, when born, do they live; into the intellect, at the time of dissolution, do they enter, do they merge.

Having realized this, he approached his father again and said: "Venerable Sir, teach me Brahman."

To him, the son, he said this: "Seek to know Brahman by means of austerities; for austerities are the means of knowing Brahman." He practiced austerities. Having practiced austerities—

Section 6. Knowledge or Bliss as Brahman

He realized that **Bliss is Brahman**; for from Bliss (Ānanda), verily, are these beings born; by bliss, when born, do they live; into bliss, at the time of dissolution, do they enter, do they merge.

This is the wisdom taught by Varuna and learnt by Bhrigu. It is established in the supreme ākāsha, the causal heart. He who knows this is established in the Bliss of Brahman. He becomes a possessor of food and an eater of food. He becomes great in offspring and cattle and in spiritual radiance and great in fame.

Sage Bhrigu finally came to realize, by himself, the basis of body, prāna, mind, intellect and Knowledge—the Supreme Being—by persistent deep thinking. He had very little help from his father.

Deep concentration of mind *is repeatedly taught by sage Varuna in order to emphasize the fact that it's the best discipline to learn any subject or to reach any goal as also mentioned in the Gita verse* ***17.03****:*

One can become whatever one wants to be, if one constantly contemplates (or visualizes) the object of desire with deep faith in God and a burning desire (**BG** 17.03). Bhagavad-Gita verse **7.19** says: Everything—Body, Prāna, mind, intellect, Knowledge etc. —is part and parcel of Brahman (वासुदेवः सर्वम् इति).

Section 7. The importance of food (i)

Let him (the knower of Brahman) never discard food; that is the duty.

The Prāna is food; body is the eater of food. The body survives on Prāna and Prāna survives in the body. Thus, one **body survives on another body. Similarly food survives on food.**

He who knows this surviving of food on food (or the **food-chain**) becomes one with God; he becomes a possessor of food and an eater of food. He becomes great in offspring and cattle and in spiritual radiance and great in fame.

Section 8. The importance of food (ii)

Let him (the knower of Brahman) never discard food; that is the duty. Water is, verily, food; fire is the eater. Fire rests on water and water rests on fire. Thus food rests/survives on food. The higher form of life uses the lower form of life as food for sustenance.

He who knows this resting of food on food is established; he becomes a possessor of food and an eater of food. He becomes great in offspring and cattle and in spiritual radiance and great in fame.

Section 9. The importance of food (iii)

Let him (the knower of Brahman) accumulate plenty of food; that is the duty.

The earth is, verily, food; the ākāsha is the eater. The ākāsha rests on the earth and the earth rests in the ākāsha. Thus food rests on food.

He who knows this resting of food on food is established; he becomes a possessor of food and an eater of food. He becomes great in offspring and cattle and in spiritual radiance and great in fame.

Section 10. Contemplation on Brahman

Let him not deny shelter to anyone: this is the duty. Therefore he should procure as much food by any legal means. To guests, he should say: "Food is ready."

3.10.01. If the food is given (to others) in the early age, food comes to the giver in the early age. If the food is given in the middle age, food comes to the giver in the middle age. If the food is given in the old age, food comes to the giver in the old age. He who knows this obtains the fruit mentioned above.

3.10.02. The Supreme resides in speech as 'well-being'; in Prāna and apāna as acquirer and preserver, in hands as actions, in the legs as movement, in the anus as excretion. This is the contemplation on Brahman through actions. (One should see Brahman behind all bodily functions)

Next follows the contemplation on Brahman, through the gods: One should meditate on Brahman as contentment (तृप्ति) in rain, as power in lightning.

3.10.03. Brahman is to be worshipped as fame in cattle, as light in the stars, as procreation, immortality and joy in the organ of generation and as everything in the ākāsha.

Let him contemplate Brahman as the support and he will be supported; let him contemplate Brahman as greatness and he will become great; let him contemplate Brahman as the mind and he will be endowed with thoughtful mind.

3.10.04. Let him contemplate on Brahman as reverence (or honor, homage) and all desires will bow down before him and pay homage. Let him contemplate Brahman as the Supreme Lord and he will be endowed with supremacy. **Let him contemplate on Brahman as the destructive agent, then all the enmity—in the enemies who hate him and also those whom he hates—will die away!**

The verses above and verse 17.03 of the Gita illustrate a great psychological truth: *'As you think, so you become'*.

3.10.05. He who knows this, as described above, after dying attains the Self which consists of food, Prāna, mind, intellect, Knowledge and bliss. Then he goes all over the globe, eating the food he desires, assuming the forms he likes and singing the glory of non-dual Brahman as follows:

3.10.06. "I am the food, I am the food, I am the food! I am the eater of the food, I am the eater of the food, I am the eater of the food! I am the uniter, I am the uniter, I am the uniter!"

"I am the first-born (food) of the True, even prior to the gods and I am immortal. He who gives away food, he alone preserves me. **I am the food that eats him who eats (improper) food." (Also see BG 3.12)**

"I, as the Supreme Lord, overpower the entire world. I am as radiant as the Sun." Whosoever knows this becomes one with Brahman. Such, indeed, is the teaching of Upanishad.

OM TAT SAT

8. AITAREYA UPANISHAD

The **Aitareya Upanishad** is one of the older, primary Upanishads commented upon by āchāryas such as Ādi Shankarāchārya and Madhvāchārya. It is a principal Upanishad, associated with the Rigveda. It deals primarily with a theory of creation and transmigration of soul. It has **30 verses written in prose.**

CHAPTER 1. THE THEORY OF CREATION

Section 1. Creation of the Jiva

1.1.01. In the beginning of a new creative cycle, called MahāKalpa lasting over 311 trillion solar years, there remains nothing but ParaBrahman (commonly known as Ātman) alone. Nothing other than Ātman exists. Ātman's inherent nature is to create the universe. (Also see MuU 1.1.08)

1.1.02. Thus it creates everything, including three worlds: the earth (भूः), the planets (भुवः), and the galaxies or heaven (स्वः).

1.1.03. Ātman thought: These indeed are the worlds I have created. Now let Me create the Lord of the Universe to control these worlds. There was water (or Nāra, the ocean of Total Energy after MahāPralaya) alone in the universe at first. In it the Lord of the Universe, Ādi Nārāyana or Cosmic Being (Purusha, shown as Shri Krishna on a Peepal leaf in the illustration on Page 78) arose.

1.1.04. Ātman contemplated over Purusha and there came out mouth. From the mouth proceeded speech, from speech fire. Then two nostrils came out. Power of smell came out of nostrils. From power of smell came air. Then two eyes burst forth; from the eyes came sight, and from sight the Sun. Ears burst forth: from the ears came out hearing. Skin burst forth from which hairs came. From the earth came herbs and trees. Then heart burst forth; from the heart came mind and from mind the Moon. Then burst forth the navel and from the navel the Apāna, from Apāna, Death. Then regenerative organ burst forth; from this organ the semen and from semen the Waters. Then He created the controlling deities (Devtās) of the organs.

Note 12: it may appear curious at first that the text described the evolving of the senses from the sense-organs and the presiding/supporting deities from the senses. But, in the evolution of a fetus, organs appear first and then the power of utilizing those organs appears and develops gradually.

Note 13: The rishis of India or even modern scientists such as Einstein have not been—or will ever be—able to give one unanimous theory of creation of the universe. The Source will, forever, remain unknown to the human mind. We find over 20 different theories of creation by various masters in the Vedas and Upanishads. Some of the theories of creation are given in **PrU** 1.04, **MuU** 1.1.07-08, **AiU** 1.1.01 and **ShU** 4.01. All theories of creation are, at best, "profound speculation". Another detailed theory of creation based on other Vedic scriptures is given for the advanced readers on:

www.gita-society.com/pdf/genesis

Darwin's theory of evolution is only very a small part of the creation theory given in the Vedas, the Bible and other scriptures. The Source creates by evolution and it takes 4.32 Billion of solar years to evolve.

Note 14: The creationists and evolutionists will not agree until they realize that both theories are not different at all. According Vedic cosmology, Lord or Mother Nature takes trillions of years to complete one cycle of creation using a slow, but perfect evolutionary process. The Creation does not and cannot happen overnight or over a week like a magic! The Darwin's theory of evolution is only a very small part of the **general theory of creation** by the power (Maya) of an unknowable God.

Section 2. Creation of Body

1.2.01. Thus Nārāyana or Cosmic person, Purusha came into worldly existence that needed a body to live in; food and water to survive.

1.2.02. The Lord brought the form of a cow and then a horse and other bodies. Devtās said, these bodies are not sufficient for them.

1.2.03. When He brought the form of a human being to them they were very pleased and accepted. He said: Enter into your respective abodes.

1.2.04-05. The deity of fire became the organ of speech and entered the mouth. Air became breath and entered the nostrils. The Sun becoming the sight entered the eyes, hearing entered the ears, the deities of herbs, plants and trees entered the soil and hair came out through human skin. The moon, becoming mind, entered the causal heart. The God of death becoming the out-breath, entered the navel. The deity of waters, becoming the semen entered the regenerative organs. Hunger and thirst entered the stomach. To whatever deity an oblation is made, hunger and thirst became sharer in it.

Section 3. Creation of Food

1.3.01. After creating the worlds and Devatās, the controlling deities or guardian angels, Lord created food for them.

1.3.02. Lord brooded over the five basic elements and food was thus produced from those five elements.

1.3.03-09. The food thus created could not be consumed by speech, eyes, ears, skin, mind or by any other organ.

1.3.10. Therefore, Apāna Vāyu (out-breath) was created to support life by food.

1.3.11-12. Lord thought how can all these survive without Me? And the creator entered creatures' body through the top of the skull to support them.

CHAPTER 2. TRANSMIGRATION OF SOUL

2.01. The soul that enters into the transmigratory cycle becomes the seed or semen. Seed is the essence gathered from all the limbs of male. Man holds his essence in his own body as semen.

2.02. The seed becomes one with the woman, just as a limb of her own. Therefore it does not hurt her, and the seed does not get rejected. She nourishes man's self that has come to her.

2.03. The mother bears the child in her womb and the father bestows his cherishing care from prenatal to pregnancy and afterwards. Son, the father's very self, is to continue the holy deeds of his father. This is the father's second birth.

2.04. The father having done his duty, departs from this world and is born again. This is father's third birth.

Note 15: it is said that just before leaving the present body the soul makes a subtle body out of subtle elements of the present physical body. It remains in this body waiting for the next reincarnation. This process is also described in the Bhagavad-Gita:

When the individual soul leaves one physical body and acquires a new physical body, He carries away the causal and subtle bodies from the physical body just as the wind carries away aroma from the flower. **(BG 15.**08)

2.05. A qualified jiva could realize the true nature of Self even inside the womb of the mother. Through the efforts of self-purification and contemplation conducted in several past lives, sage Vāmadeva was suddenly illuminated while he was still in the womb.

CHAPTER 3. MANIFESTATION OF BRAHMAN

3.01. Who is He whom we meditate upon as Ātman? Which of the two— Brahman or ParaBrahman (the Absolute or the highest Reality)?

3.02. We meditate on ParaBrahman, the Absolute or the highest Reality. It is also commonly known as Ātman by which a living being sees forms, hears sounds, smells, speaks, tastes and differentiates between right and wrong.

3.03-04. The other names of Ātman are consciousness, wisdom (Prajnā), Knowledge, power, vision, memory, recollection, desire etc. Ātman is Brahmā, Indra, all the gods, five great elements, and all those born of eggs, of womb, all the living and non-living beings. Because all these come out of Brahman and totally depend on it, thus: "All **is Brahman**". **It is said that one who realizes that consciousness (Prajnā or Chit) is Brahman (प्रज्ञानं ब्रह्म), attains immortality. (Also see BG 7.07, 7.19, IsU 01)**

OM TAT SAT

9. SHVETĀSHVATARA UPANISHAD

This Upanishad has six chapters belonging to the Shukla Yajur Veda and takes its name from the sage Shvetāshvatara. It has non-dualism as its ultimate conclusion. Still, its devotional tone is too strong to be ignored. The harmony of Knowledge and devotion is quite evident in the texts. It **has 113 verses in beautiful poetry.**

CHAPTER 1

The Ultimate Cause

1.01. Students of the Vedas discuss these questions: Is Brahman the cause of creation? Whence are we born? Why do we live? Where do we dwell at the end? Under whose orders are we subjected to the laws of happiness and misery?

1.02. Should time, or nature, or matter, or energy, or chance, or the five elements, or a combination of these be regarded as the cause? Or He who is called the purusha, the living Self?

1.03. The sages, absorbed in contemplation through one-pointed mind, discovered the creative power, belonging to the Lord hidden in His own Gunas. That non-dual Lord rules over all those causes—time, the self and the rest.

The Divine Wheel

1.04. The sages saw the Divine Wheel, which has one axis (Maya or Prakriti), a triple tyre (3 Gunas), sixteen end-parts (24 or 16 transformations of Prakriti), fifty spokes (?), twenty counter-spokes (senses and its objects) and six sets of eight (?); whose one rope (desire) is manifold; which moves on three different roads (Dharma, Artha, Kāma); and whose illusion arises from two causes (pair of opposites).

The above verse uses a highly technical (Sāmkhya type) imagery. This is a very difficult mantra to explain and to comprehend. **The universe is compared to a Divine rotating wheel** in order to indicate its dynamic nature—its perpetual motion. In the following verse the universe is compared to a river:

1.05. We can think of the universe like a river whose five currents are the five senses, which is made winding by the five elements, whose waves are the five Prānas and whose fountain-head is the mind, the source of the five forms of perception. This River has five whirlpools and its rapids are the fivefold misery; and lastly, it has many branches and five distresses (Ignorance, ego, fear of death, likes and dislikes).

1.06. In this infinite Divine wheel, in which all things abide and finally rest, the swan (Jiva) wanders about as long as jiva thinks itself different from the Controller. When grace is bestowed by Him (after he has reached the limits of self-effort) Jiva attains immortality. *(Effort precedes Grace)*

Jiva, Jagat and Jagadisha

1.07. All this is the Supreme Brahman alone. The triad of the enjoyer (Jiva), the object of enjoyment (Jagat) and the Lord (Jagadisha, Controller) is established in Him. Brahman is the immutable Source; it is imperishable. **The sages, having realized Brahman to be the essence of all changing universe, become devoted to Him. Completely merged in the Knowledge of Brahman, they attain freedom from rebirth.**

1.08. The Lord supports the perishable and the imperishable, the manifest (the effect) and the unmanifest (the cause). **The same Lord gets bound as a jiva, because of assuming the attitude of the doer and enjoyer.** The jiva when realizes the Supreme Self, is freed from all fetters.

1.09. The Supreme Lord appears as Ishvara, omniscient and omnipotent and as jiva, of limited Knowledge and power, both unborn. Apart from these two, there is another unborn prakriti (the changing Universe), which creates the idea of enjoyer, enjoyment and the object of enjoyment. Brahman is infinite and all-pervading, and therefore devoid of doership. **When the seeker realizes all these three (Jiva, Universe and Ishvara) to be Brahman, he is freed from his fetters.**

1.10. Prakriti is perishable, but God is immortal and imperishable. The non-dual Supreme Self rules both prakriti and the individual souls. Through constant contemplation on Him, by union with Him, by the Knowledge of identity with Him, one attains, in the end, cessation of all illusion of the marvelous visible universe.

1.11. When the Lord is known all fetters fall off; with the cessation of miseries, fear of birth and death come to an end. From reflection on Him there arises a state of universal lordship. And lastly, the aspirant, transcending this state also, abides in complete Knowledge and Bliss of Brahman.

1.12. The enjoyer (**jiva**), the objects of enjoyment (**jagat**) and the Ruler (Ishvara, **jagadisha**)—the triad described by the knowers of Brahman—**is nothing but Brahman. This Brahman alone, which abides within the body, should be known. Beyond it, truly, there is nothing else to be known.**

1.13. The **subtle** form of fire, that lies latent in the source (wood), is not seen; yet it is there. That very fire can be brought out by means of persistent rubbing of the wood, its source. Likewise, Ātman, which exists in all three states of consciousness like fire, can be grasped in this very body as explained below:

1.14. By making the intellect the lower piece of wood and Om the upper piece and through the practice of the friction of contemplation, one perceives the luminous Self, hidden like the fire in the wood.

1.15-16. As oil exists in sesame seeds, butter in the milk, water under the ground and fire in the wood, so the Self is realized as existing within intellect—when a man searches within again and again—by means of truthfulness, and contemplation on Brahman.

CHAPTER 2

2.01. First control the mind and senses with a view to realize the Truth. **When the Truth is found by the torch of Knowledge, the evolving soul is freed from attachment.**

2.02. When our minds are under our control, we are under the command of divine power. May He give us sufficient strength to attain the Supreme.

2.03. May the Sun-God bestow favor to the senses and the mind by joining them with the Self, so that the senses may be directed toward the Blissful Brahman and may reveal, by means of Knowledge, the mighty and radiant Brahman.

2.04. Only those rare few, who are convinced, undertake the necessary discipline and spiritual practices to realize the glory of the indwelling soul who is all-pervading, all-knowing, infinite and self-luminous.

2.05. O senses and O deities who rule them! Through salutations I unite myself with the eternal Brahman, who is also your source. Let this prayer sung by me, who follow the immortal sons of God as well as those who occupy celestial positions, hear this prayer of mine!

2.06. If sacrifices are performed without first praying to the Sun, then the mind becomes attached to sacrifices in which fire is kindled, oblations are offered to the deity Vāyu, and the juice of Soma vine is drunk excessively.

2.07. Serve the eternal Brahman with the blessings of the Sun, the cause of the universe. **Be absorbed in the thought of the eternal Brahman. Thus your work (karma) will not bind you.**

The Process of Yoga

2.08. The wise man should hold his body steady, with chest, throat and head erect; turn his senses, with the help of the mind, toward the heart and by means of the raft of Brahman, cross the fearful ocean of the world. (Also read BG 6.13-14)

2.09. The yogi of well-regulated efforts should control the Prānas; when they are quieted by the breathing process, he should breathe out through the nostrils. Then let him restrain his mind, as a charioteer restrains his vicious horses.

2.10. Let yoga be practiced in a place protected from high wind, which is level, pure and free from pebbles, gravel and fire, undisturbed by the noise of water or of market-booths and which is delightful to the mind and not offensive to the eye.

2.11. When yoga is practiced, the forms which appear first—and that gradually manifest Brahman—are: snow-flakes, smoke, sun, wind, fire, fire-flies, lightning, crystal and the moon.

2.12. When earth, water, fire, air and ākāsha arise, that is to say, when all the qualities of the five basic elements, mentioned in the books on yoga, become visible to a yogi after attaining yogic perfection, then the yogi's body becomes purified by the fire of yoga and he is freed from illness, old age or death.

2.13. The precursors of perfection in yoga, they say, are lightness and healthiness of the body, absence of desire, clear complexion, pleasant voice, sweet odor and slight excretions.

2.14. As gold covered by dirt shines bright after it has been cleaned; similarly, the yogi upon realizing the truth of Ātman becomes one with the non-dual Ātman, attains the goal and shines by becoming free from grief.

2.15. When the yogi realizes the real nature of Brahman in this body—by the Knowledge of the Self—as a radiant lamp; then, having known the unborn and immutable Lord, who is untouched by ignorance and its effects, **he is freed from all fetters.**

Lord Krishna said: Self-knowledge is the only goal of all spiritual practices, O Arjuna. (BG 4.33)

Description of the Glory of God

2.16. This Divinity pervades all directions in their entirety. He is the first-born (Brahmā or HiranyaGarbha). He has entered into the womb. He alone is born as a child, and is to be born in future. He is inside all persons as the Indwelling Self and His face is everywhere.

2.17. Salutations to that Divinity who is in the fire, who is in the water, who is in the plants, who is in the trees, and who has pervaded the entire universe.

CHAPTER 3

3.01. It is the non-dual Self that exists at all times—before and during the creation and after dissolution of the universe. It assumes manifold powers and appears as the Divine Lord by virtue of His unfathomable power of maya. He is the protector of all the worlds and controls all the various forces working therein. Those who realize this Being, become immortal.

Rudra is another name of Ishvara

3.02. Rudra or the Self is only One; for the knowers of Brahman do not admit the existence of a second, He alone rules all the worlds by His powers. He dwells as the inner self in every living being. After having created all the worlds, He, their Protector, takes them back into Himself at the time of great dissolution (महाप्रलय).

3.03. His eyes, faces, arms, and feet are everywhere. He endows men with arms and feet, birds with legs and wings. Having produced heaven and earth, He remains as their non-dual manifester.

3.04. He is the omniscient Rudra, the creator of the gods, the bestower of their powers, and the supporter of the universe. He, who in the beginning, gave birth to Hiranyagarbha (Brahmā), may endow us with clear intellect!

3.05. O Rudra, You dwell in the body and bestow happiness! Look upon us with your most blessed form, which is auspicious, non-terrifying and all good.

3.06. O Dweller in the body and bestower of happiness, make gentle that arrow which You hold in Your hand ready to shoot, O Protector of the body! Do not injure man nor the beast!

(Rudra is the destructive power of God.)

Personal and impersonal aspects of Brahman

3.07. The Supreme Lord is higher than Brahmā and even beyond Brahman. He is vast and hidden in the bodies of all living beings. **By knowing Him, who alone pervades the entire universe, one become immortal.**

3.08. I know that great Purusha, who is luminous like the sun and beyond darkness. Only by knowing Him does one pass over death; there is no other way to reach the Supreme Goal.

3.09. The whole universe is pervaded by Purusha, to whom there is nothing superior, from whom there is nothing different, than whom there is nothing either smaller or greater; who stands alone, motionless as a tree and established in His own glory.

3.10. That Being is far beyond this world, is without form and without misery. They who know Him become immortal; but others, indeed, suffer pain.

3.11. All faces are His faces; all heads, His heads; all necks, His necks. He dwells in the causal hearts of all beings. He is the all-pervading Bhagavān. Therefore He is the omnipresent and merciful Lord.

3.12. He, indeed, is the great Purusha, the Lord of creation, preservation and destruction, who inspires the mind to attain the state of stainlessness. He is the Ruler and the imperishable Light.

3.13. The Purusha, no bigger than a thumb, is the inner Self, ever seated in the causal heart of all creatures. He is known by the intellect which is purified by Knowledge and is perceived in the causal heart. They who know Him become immortal.

The supreme can be described only by Parables

3.14. That infinite Purusha has many heads, eyes, feet, and envelopes the whole universe. And yet He is very close residing in our causal heart.

3.15. The Purusha alone is all this—what has been and what will be. He is also the Lord of immortality and of the universe.

3.16. His hands and feet are everywhere; His eyes, heads and faces are everywhere; His ears are everywhere; He exists pervading everything in the universe.

The Supreme Being has His hands, feet, eyes, head, mouth, and ears everywhere, because He is all-pervading and omnipresent. **(BG 13.**13-14)

3.17. Himself devoid of human senses, He shines through the functions of all the senses. He is the capable ruler of all; He is the shelter of all and the friend of all.

3.18. It is He who resides in the body, the city of nine gates. He is the soul that sports in the outside world. He is the master of the whole world, animate and inanimate.

The human body has been called the City of Nine Gates (or openings) in the scriptures. The nine openings are: Two openings each for the eyes, ears, and nose; and one each for the mouth, anus, and urethra. The Lord of all beings and the universe who resides in this city along with the individual soul or the living entity (Jiva) is called the Spiritual Being (Purusha) performing and directing all action. (**BG** 5.13) The Lord— being unattached to material Nature—remains free as a mere witness of the cosmic play.

3.19. Without hands and feet He goes fast and grasps; without eyes He sees; without ears He hears. He knows whatever is to be known, yet there is none who knows Him. They say He is the foremost, the great Infinite Being.

The Supreme Being walks without legs, hears without ears, performs many actions without hands, smells without a nose, sees without eyes, speaks without a mouth, and enjoys all tastes without a tongue. All His actions are so marvelous that one finds His greatness utterly beyond description.

3.20. Subtler than the subtlest and greater than the greatest, the Ātman is concealed in the causal heart of all creatures. By earning the grace of the Creator, one becomes free from sorrows and desires, and then realizes Him as the great Lord.

3.21. Know Him as the non-decaying, primeval One, the Self of all things; which, being all-pervading, exists everywhere, and which the wise declare to be free from birth and death. The teachers of Brahman, indeed, speak of it as eternal.

CHAPTER 4

4.01. May that Divine Being—though Himself formless, gives rise to various forms in different ways with the help of His own power,

for His own unknowable purpose, and who dissolves the entire universe in Himself in the end—endow us with good thoughts!

4.02. The Divine Being Himself is the fire, the sun, the air, the moon, the starry sky, the waters, the Cosmic manifestation (virāt) and Prajāpati, Brahmā.

4.03. You are woman, You are man; You are youth and the maiden. You are an old man tottering along with a staff; **it's You alone who assume diverse forms.**

4.04. You are the dark-blue butterfly; You are the green parrot with red eyes; You are the thunder-cloud, the seasons and all the oceans. You are beginningless and all-pervading. From You all the worlds manifest.

4.05. There is a single, unborn Female (prakriti) of red, white and black colors (the three Gunas) which gives birth to many individual souls (Jiva). Some individual souls (Jiva) enjoy Her and become attached to Her, while other individual souls enjoy Her and then leave Her after discovering the uselessness of worldly pleasures.

The Parable of Two Birds

4.06. Two birds (Jiva and Ishvara) of beautiful feathers, who are inseparable friends, reside on the same body-tree. One of them eats the fruits of the tree and enjoys, while the other looks on as a witness without eating. (Also see MuU 3.1.01)

4.07. Sitting on the same tree of life, the individual soul (Jiva) gets entangled and becomes miserable; being deluded on account of **forgetting his real divine nature.** When he sees the other, the Lord of all, whom all devotees worship, and realizes that all glory is His (and not that of jiva), then Jiva is relieved of his misery.

4.08. Of what use are the Vedas to him who does not know the indestructible, highest divine Being, in whom the gods and the Vedas reside? Only those who know This Being attain bliss.

4.09. The Lord of maya projects sacrifices, spiritual practices, past and future, religious observances, all that the Vedas declare, and the whole world including ourselves. It is in this world that Brahman as the jiva gets entangled by maya (and tries to get out of it!).

4.10. Know that Prakriti is maya and that Great God is the Lord of maya. **The whole universe is filled with objects which are His parts and parcel.**

The way to the Supreme

4.11. One attains infinite peace on realizing that self-effulgent Adorable Lord, the bestower of blessings, who, though one, presides over all the various aspects of Brahmā, and in whom this entire universe dissolves, and from which it appears again and again in manifold forms.

4.12. May He—who created the gods and supports them; who witnessed the birth of the cosmic mind (Brahmā or HiranyaGarbha); who confers bliss and wisdom to the devotees, destroying their sins and sorrows, and punishing all breachers of The Law (of karma), the great seer and the Lord of all—endow us with good thoughts!

4.13. He who is the Lord of the gods, in whom the worlds find their support, who rules over all two-footed and four-footed beings—let us serve the supreme God who is radiant and blissful, with an oblation.

4.14. By knowing Him—who is subtler than the subtlest, who organized an orderly universe from scatter (rabble, chaos, void),[**] who takes various forms without undergoing any real change, the creator of all, who pervades the universe and is all auspicious—one attains the supreme peace. (Also see **ShU** 5.13)

[**] This verse seems to refer to the Big Bang theory when there was rabble, disorder, void and chaos in the space before creative cycle began! The word '**Kalila**' could also mean amidst huge difficulties.

4.15. He alone is the protector of the world at the proper time. He is the lord of the universe hidden in all creatures. In Him the divine sages and the gods merge. Realizing Him thus, one cuts asunder the fetters of death.

4.16. One is released from all fetters on realizing the Blissful One who envelops the world, and who hides Himself in all beings in an extremely subtle form, as butter—the essence of milk—hides in the milk.

4.17. This Divinity, who created the universe and who pervades everything, always dwells in the causal hearts of creatures; becoming individualized by emotions, intellect, will and imagination. Those who realize this become immortal.

4.18. When ignorance is dispelled, there is neither day nor night, neither being nor non-being. There is only that Auspicious One who is imperishable, and who is worthy of being adored by Brahmā, the creator. From Him has proceeded all the ancient wisdom which has come down to us in the form of the Vedas.

4.19. No one can comprehend Him in any way. There is none equal to or greater than Him. His name is Great Glory.

4.20. His form does not come within the range of the senses. No one perceives Him with the eye. Those who know Him, through the faculty of intuition, as seated in their causal heart, become immortal.

4.21. Because You are birthless; some souls, frightened by birth and death, take refuge in You—wishing Your help in getting out of the cycle of birth and death. O Rudra, may Your compassionate heart protect us!

4.22. O Rudra, do not destroy our children and grand children. Do not destroy our lives; do not destroy our cows or horses; do not destroy good people by Your anger. We invoke Thee always, with oblations, for our protection.

CHAPTER 5

5.01. In the Immutable, infinite Supreme Brahman remain hidden the two: Knowledge and ignorance. Ignorance leads to worldliness and Knowledge to immortality. Brahman, who controls both Knowledge and ignorance, is different from both.

5.02. He alone presides over Nature in all aspects and controls all forms and all sources of production (योनि). He witnesses the birth of the first born seer of golden color (HiranyaGarbha, the Golden Egg, Brahmā) and gives him Knowledge and wisdom.

5.03. Creating a network of different species and sub-species within a biological kingdom or domain, the Supreme Being withdraws them into their source and brings them forth again and again. The Great Self holds control over all of them.

5.04. Just as the sun shines lighting up all space above, below and across, so also the adorable God—the repository of all goodness and greatness—presides over everything and is the **cause of all causes** (सर्वकारण कारणम्).

5.05. He who is the one source of the world, brings everything out of Himself, and leads creatures to perfection according to their karma. He endows each being with its distinguishing characteristics and presides over the entire universe.

5.06. He lies hidden in the teachings of Upanishads, which form the essence of the Vedas. Lord Brahmā knows Him as the source of himself and the Vedas. Those gods and seers who realized Him in former days became identified with Him, and verily became immortal.

Reasons for the reincarnation of jiva

5.07. Endowed with three Gunas, jiva performs actions and seeks its fruits; it reaps the fruit of what it has done. Taking various forms led by the Gunas, jiva roams around the wheel of transmigration—according to its deeds. (Also see **BG** 8.24-26 and 14.18)

5.08. He is subtle and pure, effulgent and infinite like the sun, He alone is seen becoming another entity (individual soul or Jiva), equal to the size of a thumb on account of the finiteness of the causal heart in which He appears. Jiva associates himself with the ego and choice due to limitations of his past deeds.

5.09. That individual soul (Jiva) is as subtle as a hair point divided and sub-divided hundreds of times. Yet he is potentially infinite.

5.10. Jiva is neither female, nor male, nor neuter. It becomes identified with whatever body it assumes.

5.11. By means of desire, attachment and delusion, the embodied soul takes successive various forms in various places according to his deeds. Just as the body develops when nourished by food and drink, **Jiva develops by its own effort and attains the highest destiny.**

5.12. The embodied soul/ spirit (or Jiva) chooses many forms, gross and subtle, based on the qualities of his previous body, mind and actions. Yet another cause of their choice is God, the all-knowing and controller who keeps records of karma, helps and guides the individual in his choice.

5.13. By realizing Him—who is without beginning or end, who creates cosmos in the midst of (chaos and) huge difficulties, who assumes various forms, the creator of all things, who is the non-dual pervader of the universe and Divine Being—one is freed from all fetters. (Also see **ShU** 4.14)

5.14. That Supreme Divinity, who created both Energy and Matter, is the source of all arts and sciences; and is intuitively perceived by a pure and devoted mind. After realizing Him—as the blissful, nameless and formless—one is freed from further embodiment.

CHAPTER 6

6.01. Some deluded thinkers speak of Nature, and others of time, as the force that revolves this Divine wheel of creation. **The creation is the Glory of God manifested in the form of the universe!**

6.02. It should be known that a very small fraction of His divine energy (Teja) takes various forms such as: Ether, air, fire, water, and earth at His command. He is the master of three Gunas and the maker of time, who is omniscient, who is pure consciousness, and **all this is made up of His energy.**

6.03. After setting the creation in motion and withdrawing (by remaining aloof as a mere witness) Himself from it, He unites the principle of Spirit with the principle of Matter—with one (Consciousness), with two (duality), with three (Gunas) and with eight (elements)—with the help of time and their own inherent properties.

6.04. He who attains purity of mind by performing actions as an offering to the Lord and attaching prakriti and all its effects to Brahman, realizes his true Self and thereby transcends the physical world. In the absence of Gunas, all his past karma are destroyed. And after paying off the prārabdha karma (or fate) he attains final Liberation.

6.05. The Great Lord is the origin and the cause that unites the soul with the body. He is above the three divisions of time (past, present and future) and is seen to be **without any real part**. When one knows the adorable God dwelling in the causal heart, taking many forms and as the Source of all things—one attains final liberation.

6.06. He from whom this universe manifests is higher and other than all forms as well as time. When one knows Him—who is the indweller, the bringer of good, the destroyer of evil, the Lord of all powers, the immortal support of all—one attains final liberation.

6.07. May we realize Him who is the Supreme Lord of lords, the Supreme Deity of deities, the Ruler of rulers (gods). He is the self-luminous, adorable Lord of the universe.

6.08. He is without a body or organs. No one is equal or superior to Him. The Vedas speak of His transcendental form and powers, which are inherent and capable of producing diverse effects, and also of His omniscience and might.

6.09. No one in the world is His master, no one has any control over Him. **There is no way to prove His existence.** He is the cause of all causes, and the ruler of individual souls. He has no parent, nor is there anyone who is His lord.

Lord is the efficient and material cause of creation

6.10. May the Supreme Lord—who **covers Himself by the products of His own maya, the material world**; just as a female spider does with the threads drawn from its own navel—grant us merger in Brahman!

As a female spider spreads out the web from within, plays in it, and again draws the web into itself, similarly the Eternal Being (or Spirit) creates the material world from itself, plays in it as living entity, and takes it into itself during complete dissolution. All manifestations are born, sustained, and finally merge in Spirit as bubbles of water are born, sustained, and merge in water. Spirit manifests itself into the universe by using its own internal power without the help of any external help. It is possible for one Spirit—by virtue of possessing diverse powers—to be transformed into multiplicity without any outside help. The Eternal Being is thus both the efficient and the material cause of creation.

6.11. God, who is the One only, is **hidden in all beings**. He is all-pervading, and is the inner self of all creatures. He presides over

all actions, and all beings reside in Him. He is the witness, and He is the Pure Consciousness free from the three Gunas of Nature.

6.12. To those wise men who ever feel the presence of God—who is the ruler of all, and who makes the one seed (prakriti) diversify—belongs eternal happiness, and to none else.

6.13. He is the Eternal among the eternal and the Intelligent among all that are intelligent. Though one, He grants the desires of many. One is released from all fetters on realizing Him as the cause of all. He is realized through philosophy and religious disciplines.

Brahman is the light of all lights

6.14. The sun does not shine there; neither the moon, nor the stars. These lights do not shine there—much less this fire. **Because He shines, everything shines after Him. By His light all this shines.** (Also see KaU 5.15 and BG **15.06**)

The way to the Supreme

6.15. The only destroyer of ignorance in the midst of this universe, He alone is in the fire and also in the water. Those who realize Him overcome death. There is no other way to reach the Supreme Goal.

6.16. He is the creator of everything as well as the knower of everything. He is His own source, He is all-knowing, and He is the Author of time. He is the repository of all good qualities, and the master of all sciences. He is the controller of both Matter and Spirit, and the lord of the Gunas. He is the cause of liberation from cycle of birth and death, and also of bondage which results in continuance of the cycles of birth and death.

6.17. He is the soul of the universe, He is immortal and He is the ruler. He is the all-knowing, the all-pervading, the protector of the universe, and the eternal ruler. None else is there efficient to govern the world eternally.

6.18-19. He who in the beginning of creation created Brahmā and delivered the Vedas to him; who constitutes the supreme bridge to immortality, who is the **partless**, free from actions, tranquil, faultless, taintless and without ignorance. Seeking liberation, I take refuge in that Effulgent One, who's light of grace aids the understanding of Ātman.

6.20. Only when men can roll up the sky like a paper, will there be an end of misery for them without realizing God.

Any effort to be free from misery without realizing God, is as futile as an attempt to roll up the sky!

6.21. Himself realizing Brahman by the power of self-control and concentration of mind, as well as by the grace of God, sage Shvetāshvatara explained—to the highest order of Samnyāsins—the truth of that supremely holy Brahman sought by all the seers.

6.22. The profound Knowledge of Vedānta was taught in the former age. It should not be given to one whose passions (Rajo Guna) have not been subdued, nor to one who is not a worthy son or a worthy disciple.

6.23. These truths, when taught, will surely shine forth only in that high-minded person who has supreme devotion to God and an equal degree of devotion to the spiritual master.

OM TAT SAT

Read all 108 upanishads: www.gita-society.com/pdf/108upanishads.pdf

ACKNOWLEDGMENTS

The valuable editing help provided by Peter Hansmann is gratefully acknowledged.

References used:

(1) The Upanishads, Translated by F. Max Müller, 1879

(2) Shri RamaKrishna MaTh Publications on Upanishads by Swami Sharvananda and Swami Nikhilananda.

(3) Adi Shankarachārya, Swami Chinmayananda and others' commentaries on the Upanishads on the web.

(4) www.ishwar.com, with permission from Ishwar Joshi

upanishads-9/pooja.../pooja11.05x8.3-workingIGSvyas2bkrishna2.pdf
9upanishads116pg.pdf jan 2016